T0323899

MICROECONOMICS
THE BASICS

Microeconomics: The Basics is an accessible introduction to the core topics in the field. Intended for those with little or no background in the subject, it provides the reader with a solid foundation of the basic principles of microeconomics and establishes a framework for further study.

Topics in the book cover the most important areas in microeconomics, including supply and demand, consumer choice, elasticity, market failure and the role of government, production and cost, perfect competition, monopoly, oligopoly, monopolistic competition, the labor market, and capital and financial markets. Applications that are relevant for contemporary study of the field are also included. Written in a highly engaging style, each chapter is accompanied by key terminology lists to emphasize important terms and concepts, as well as further reading suggestions which provide the opportunity for students to read more about specific topics, with a glossary provided at the end of the book.

Microeconomics: The Basics is essential reading for anyone who wishes to master the fundamental principles of microeconomics.

Thomas R. Sadler is Professor of Economics at Western Illinois University. He teaches courses on the Fundamentals of Economic Theory, Environmental Economics, Energy Economics, Labor Economics, and the Chicago Economy. His research focuses on environmental policy, energy economics, professional sports leagues, and high-performance organizations.

The Basics Series

The Basics is a highly successful series of accessible guidebooks which provide an overview of the fundamental principles of a subject area in a jargon-free and undaunting format.

Intended for students approaching a subject for the first time, the books both introduce the essentials of a subject and provide an ideal springboard for further study. With over 50 titles spanning subjects from artificial intelligence (AI) to women's studies, *The Basics* are an ideal starting point for students seeking to understand a subject area.

Each text comes with recommendations for further study and gradually introduces the complexities and nuances within a subject.

For more information about this series, please visit: www.routledge.com/The-Basics/book-series/B

MICROECONOMICS

THE BASICS

Thomas R. Sadler

Routledge
Taylor & Francis Group

LONDON AND NEW YORK

Designed cover image: mfto / DigitalVision Vectors / Getty Images®

First published 2025
by Routledge
4 Park Square, Milton Park, Abingdon, Oxon OX14 4RN

and by Routledge
605 Third Avenue, New York, NY 10158

Routledge is an imprint of the Taylor & Francis Group, an informa business

British Library Cataloguing-in-Publication Data
A catalog record for this book is available from the British Library

Library of Congress Cataloging-in-Publication Data
Names: Sadler, Thomas R., author.
Title: Microeconomics : the basics / Thomas R. Sadler.
Description: Abingdon, Oxon ; New York, NY : Routledge, 2025. | Series: Routledge - the basics | Includes bibliographical references and index.
Identifiers: LCCN 2024032725 | ISBN 9781032875330 (hardback) | ISBN 9781032875309 (paperback) | ISBN 9781003533115 (ebook)
Subjects: LCSH: Microeconomics.
Classification: LCC HB172 .S126 2025 | DDC 338.5--dc23/eng/20240918
LC record available at https://lccn.loc.gov/2024032725

ISBN: 978-1-032-87533-0 (hbk)
ISBN: 978-1-032-87530-9 (pbk)
ISBN: 978-1-003-53311-5 (ebk)

DOI: 10.4324/9781003533115

Typeset in Bembo
by SPi Technologies India Pvt Ltd (Straive)

Access the Support Material: www.routledge.com/9781032875309

To Holly, Maya, and Mathew with love.

CONTENTS

FIGURES

TABLES

ACKNOWLEDGMENTS

I thank Routledge for publishing this book. At every step of the writing process, Chloe Herbert and Michelle Gallagher provided helpful feedback and encouragement. It is a pleasure working with such responsive partners in the publishing process.

Professionally, I benefit from the interaction with many colleagues, including Tara Feld, Jessica Lin, Manda Tiwari, Braxton Gately, Alla Melkumian, Haritima Chauhan, and Jobu Babin. Thank you for our ongoing conversations about economics and life.

Personally, I enjoy the support from a wonderful family, including Judy, Charles, Laura, Chris, Mark, Fred, and Rick.

I dedicate this book and all of my work to Holly, Maya, and Mathew. I love you very much.

AN OVERVIEW OF THE BOOK

The book includes three parts. Chapter 1 introduces the topic of microeconomics. Part I addresses markets, consumer choice, and government, including supply and demand (Chapter 2), economic efficiency, market failure, and the role of government (Chapter 3), elasticity (Chapter 4), and consumer choice (Chapter 5). Part II considers the theory of the firm, including production, cost, and profit (Chapter 6), perfect competition (Chapter 7), monopoly (Chapter 8), oligopoly (Chapter 9), and monopolistic competition (Chapter 10). Part III discusses labor, capital, and financial markets, including the labor market (Chapter 11) and capital and financial markets (Chapter 12). In Part III, instructors may cover the chapters in either order.

INTRODUCTION TO MICROECONOMICS

SCARCITY, CHOICE, AND PRODUCTION

Microeconomics is the field of study that addresses how individuals, households, and firms make decisions and how those decisions interact. Examples include how individuals choose to allocate their money for the purchase of goods and services or how firms choose to maximize profit. These decisions would be straightforward if individuals and firms did not experience constraints. However, these economic agents must work with the principles of *scarcity* and *choice*.

Scarcity exists because the *economic resources* that produce output do not exist in an unlimited supply. For example, when producing cell phones, firms employ economic resources, including *land* (the resources that come from nature, including water and fossil fuels), *labor* (effort of workers), *physical capital* (machinery, equipment, and manufactured goods that make other goods and services), and *entrepreneurship* (the owners or managers of firms that assume risk and attempt to profit from production).

Because firms have to pay to employ economic resources, choices must occur. A firm producing cell phones may decide to substitute physical capital for labor resources, attempting to reduce the cost of production and increase productivity. If all firms in an *industry*—a group of firms that produce the same or similar goods and services—make the same choice to reduce the number of workers, the result will be a higher level of unemployment. However, the opposite

DOI: 10.4324/9781003533115-1

form of substitution may occur: firms producing output such as computer games and other services may substitute labor for physical capital, employing more workers in an attempt to generate creative ideas in the production process. The result may be a lower level of unemployment.

Economists use models as tools of analysis. Because models are representations of reality, they help economists analyze important issues and problems. In economic models, economists use figures and equations to learn about the economy and human behavior. Good models are flexible and simple, helping economists forecast how changes in certain variables may impact consumer decision-making, production, or other choices. An economic model, however, does not include all aspects of reality but only the details that allow an understanding of the relationship between key variables. As a result, economic models establish assumptions about the variables that are included and how economic agents make decisions. Economic models assume that consumers make rational decisions, balancing the costs and benefits of different choices. But, in reality, consumers may not always make rational decisions because of advertising or impulse buying.

The circular flow model serves as an example of an economic model. It demonstrates the role of firms, households, and markets in the economy. The simplified version assumes that firms and households are the main decision-makers. A more complete version of the model includes the government and foreign sectors. In the model, two markets—an output market with goods and services and a factor market with economic resources—organize economic activity.

In Figure 1.1, the simplified version of the model, households consume goods and services and provide economic resources. Household consumption leads to spending, while work generates income. By hiring economic resources, firms produce and sell output, generating revenue. The act of employing economic resources creates income in the form of wages to workers, rent to owners of capital, and profit to entrepreneurs. The markets enable a continuous circular flow. But disruptions may occur. Pandemics hinder the ability of firms to produce. Negative household sentiments lead to reductions in spending. Economic downturns increase unemployment. In different contexts, positive influences may exist. The point

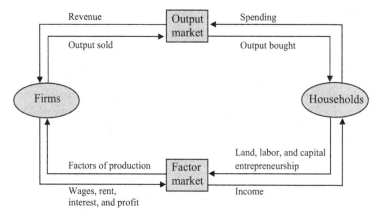

Figure 1.1 Circular flow model

is that the model demonstrates how economic resources produce output, and how income is generated for firms and households.

PRINCIPLES OF ECONOMICS

In the field of economics, several important principles exist. First, when economic agents make decisions, they experience *tradeoffs*. College students must decide how to allocate their time between studying and leisure. For most students, allocating more time for studying leads to higher grades. But the tradeoff is less time available for other activities. Every hour allocated to studying means one less hour available for friends, organizations, or social media. With families, a tradeoff exists with the allocation of income for savings. When families save more, they have less income available for current consumption. But they will have more money available for future consumption. For societies, a tradeoff exists between the implementation of laws that reduce the flow of greenhouse gases into the atmosphere and higher business income. When these environmental laws require firms to alter their production processes, use a different combination of economic resources, or implement renewable forms of energy, production costs rise, profits fall, and less money is available for wages and salaries. But, over time, the environmental and health benefits of a cleaner environment lead to economic gains.

For society, a tradeoff may also exist between *efficiency* and *equity*. When society receives the maximum amount of benefits from the use of scarce resources, an efficient allocation occurs. The outcome is an increase in the size of the economic pie. When the benefits of the economic pie are uniformly divided among members of society, an equal allocation exists. Economic growth, however, may increase the size of the economic pie, but those at the higher end of the income distribution may receive most of the benefits.

Second, *opportunity cost* is the value of the best foregone alternative. When individuals decide to study more, save less, or value the future, they give up the opportunity to choose a different option. In this context, making one decision over another requires the consideration of both costs and benefits. As an example, the benefits of going to college include becoming a more educated person, developing academic skills, and improving job prospects. But the costs include more than the price of tuition (individuals must pay for room and board whether they go to college or not). The opportunity cost of a college education entails the value of the best foregone alternative. For most students, the opportunity cost is the lost income from working full time. When students choose not to work in order to take classes and experience college life, they give up the ability to maintain full-time wages.

As another example, an opportunity cost exists when students choose to study more. A tradeoff exists between studying and having more time for other activities (Table 1.1). Suppose a student has 20 hours available each week to allocate between studying and leisure activities, such as clubs, intramural sports, or socializing. More study time leads to a higher grade point average (GPA) but less time for leisure activities. If a student is studying enough to earn a 3.0 GPA and wants to raise it to 4.0, the question becomes one of opportunity cost (Figure 1.2). What is the opportunity cost of this

Table 1.1 Study time and GPA

	(a)	(b)	(c)	(d)	(e)
Study time (hours)	0	5	10	15	20
GPA	0	1.0	2.0	3.0	4.0

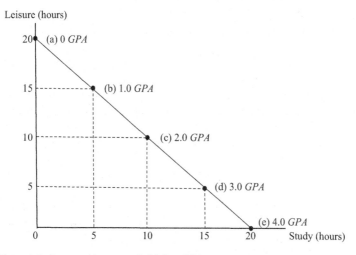

Figure 1.2 Opportunity cost of a higher GPA

decision? The answer is five hours of lost leisure time, a movement from bundle (d) to bundle (e).

Third, people respond to the *incentives* that induce specific responses. Rational individuals consider the costs and benefits of their actions. Properly crafted incentives impact benefits or costs, nudging individuals in one way or another. In a market, if the price of automobiles decreases, all else equal, the quantity demanded by consumers increases. At the same time, the quantity supplied by producers decreases. In this example, a change in market price impacts the demand and supply decisions.

However, public policy provides the incentive for firms to alter the automobiles that are produced. A tax on gasoline, common at the state or national level, increases the price at the pump. This policy provides the incentive for consumers to substitute away from fuel-inefficient vehicles to those that are more fuel-efficient, such as hybrids or electric cars. By altering the mix of vehicles on the road, the government may establish a policy goal of fighting climate change or generating tax revenue. Another aspect of this policy exists: if a higher price on gasoline discourages certain behavior, individuals may choose alternative forms of transportation, such as buses for shorter trips or trains for longer trips. As a result, when studying incentives, it is important to consider both direct and indirect effects.

Fourth, rational individuals think at the margin. Marginal analysis entails a comparison of the additional benefits and costs that occur with a choice. For example, when making production decisions, firms attempt to maximize profit. But they produce more output if marginal revenue (MR; the revenue from producing one more unit of output) exceeds the marginal cost (MC; the cost from producing one more unit of output). As a result, firms will continue to produce output until $MR = MC$. The reason is that this is the point of profit maximization.

When individuals make decisions, they use marginal analysis. Suppose an individual is deciding whether or not to consume an additional cookie. The marginal benefit (MB) of this choice is the additional satisfaction that comes from eating another cookie. The MC is the price, plus any discomfort that results from the decision. When the individual consumes more cookies, MB declines: satisfaction decreases with additional units of consumption. But MC increases. In the presence of a constant price, the individual's level of discomfort rises when eating beyond an optimal level of consumption. In this example, how many cookies should the rational individual consume? The individual should consume to the point where $MB = MC$. But beyond that point, $MC > MB$: the consumption of additional cookies would create more cost than benefit.

Fifth, *trade*, the voluntary exchange between economic agents, improves the position of those involved in the transaction. A smartphone producer may experience costs of $500 in the manufacturing process, sell the smartphone to a retailer for $800, and create a per-unit profit. The retailer may sell it to a consumer for $1,000, also earning a profit. The consumer may think this is a good price, willing to spend even more for the product. With this transaction, each agent experiences gains from trade.

HOW ECONOMIES OPERATE

The circular flow model demonstrates that markets facilitate the transformation of economic resources into goods and services, a process that generates income for both households and firms. The economy coordinates productive activities. The incentives inherent in the output and factor markets ensure that economic resources flow to productive uses. Efficient outcomes result. If technological advance creates products in high demand in one sector of the economy, higher wages will attract workers. In contrast, economic sectors that do not evolve according to changing economic conditions will experience declining profits.

In a *market economy*, individual choice and market incentives guide decision-making. There is no economic coordinator that determines the flow of economic resources to one sector or another. Markets guide these flows. In particular, demand-side (consumer) and supply-side (producer) decisions establish market prices and how the prices change over time. A market economy provides consumers with the choice of which goods and services to purchase. At the same time, producers have the choice of which goods and services to bring to the market. Market economies create efficient but potentially inequitable outcomes.

In a *mixed economy*, both the public sector (government) and private sector (firms) contribute to economic activity. Government spending flows to public services, the provision of public goods, the maintenance of public utilities, and many other activities. Governments allocate resources to public education, police and fire protection, and highways. In practice, economies are normally mixed, but the level of *government intervention*—when the government alters the decisions of individuals, groups, or firms—depends on the preferences for public goods, an equitable income distribution, and policies that correct market inefficiencies.

Market failure occurs when a free market creates an undesirable outcome. Markets normally allocate economic resources efficiently, creating an optimal distribution of output. However, markets may fail to provide an optimal outcome. Markets may also set a price that is too high or too low from society's perspective. Four examples of market failure exist.

First, when external costs or benefits are present, markets do not produce the optimal level of output. An external cost or benefit is something that accrues to individuals not involved in market activity. With an external cost such as pollution damage, the free market sets a price that is too low and a level of output that is too high.

With an external benefit such as society's gain from public education, both the market price and level of output are too low. In these examples, public policy may correct for externalities.

Second, if markets have a large number of sellers, individual sellers do not influence the market price. However, if a market experiences a lack of competition, a single seller may increase price while maintaining its market position. In the absence of government intervention, this represents a suboptimal outcome.

Third, when the buyer and seller do not share the same information, market failure occurs. With *asymmetric information*, a seller may know more than a buyer about a good or service, such as in the market for pre-owned vehicles. If asymmetric information occurs, the market may set prices that are too high.

Fourth, with the provision of public goods, market failure may occur. The market provides the private goods produced by firms, setting prices and quantities and allocating the benefits of consumption to individuals. Examples are the goods and services that consumers purchase in stores or online. But public goods are not exclusive (no market prices) and not rivalrous (available to all). Because of a lack of profit with public goods—such as bridges, national defense, and public schools—the market underproduces them. A problem that arises with public goods is the potential for free riding when individuals enjoy the benefits from a public good but do not incur the costs. An example is when individuals benefit from herd immunity from a vaccine but do not receive the vaccine. In this case, the government may require vaccinations.

Market failure provides an incentive for government intervention. Because market failure leads to a suboptimal outcome, government intervention may correct the problem, moving the market to an optimal position. In the case of externalities, the government may establish a price for a negative externality (environmental tax for pollution damage) or a subsidy for a positive externality (student grants or loans for public education). With a market that lacks competition, the government may regulate the firm that is producing output, ensuring that price gouging does not occur. In the presence of asymmetric information, the government may require the provision of information to everyone in the market. With public goods, the government may provide them directly or establish an incentive to firms for their provision.

A caveat about government intervention relates to cost. Firms have the incentive to minimize the cost of production. This choice corresponds to profit maximization. In the market, competition guarantees cost-minimizing behavior. With a coffee shop, for example, wasteful spending reduces the ability of the business to compete in the market. But the government does not have a profit motive. The implication is that the government may not minimize costs.

From an economic perspective, government intervention is justified on the basis of eliminating market inefficiencies. But no guarantee exists that government intervention will achieve this goal. If the government intervenes and reduces market inefficiency, the intervention is successful. If intervention worsens the inefficiency, *government failure* exists. When the cost of government intervention is less than the value of the efficiency gain, intervention exists as the best solution.

ECONOMIC ANALYSIS

Microeconomics is about understanding how economic agents make decisions. Microeconomists study the motivations of economic agents and how they respond to incentives. With this analysis, it is possible to evaluate the decisions of consumers and firms. The question is how to maximize the satisfaction from consumption given a budget constraint (consumers) or maximize the profit from production given a cost constraint (firms). How should consumers allocate a budget between different consumption alternatives? To maximize profit, how many units of output should firms produce? These and other questions are fundamental to the study of microeconomics.

A difference exists between *positive analysis* and *normative analysis*. Positive analysis addresses economics without subjective judgments. The statement that an individual has $15 to spend on lunch is objective. The statement, however, that an individual should spend all of the money on a specific lunch item is an example of normative analysis, what ought to happen. Debates over policy implementation often adopt a subjective framework if the analyst argues for one policy over another.

In addition to model building, economists simplify their analysis through the implementation of the economic principles in this chapter, including tradeoffs, opportunity cost, incentives, marginal analysis, and trade. But economic analysis normally demonstrates what happens when one variable changes, holding other variables constant. This is the *ceteris paribus* assumption when other things remain equal. The ceteris paribus assumption contributes to the formulation of economic theory.

But sometimes the ceteris paribus assumption does not hold. If the price decreases, future expectations may change. At the same time, household income may fall, altering consumption patterns. As a result, an economic theory does not mean that it is always correct, but that it is useful in forecasting the behavior of economic agents. When an economic theory differs from reality, the empirical result is interesting and noteworthy. To address these areas of economic analysis, the book is organized in three parts.

Part I addresses markets and government. Chapter 2 builds the most important model in the field of economics: supply and demand. Markets bring together buyers and sellers for the purpose of exchange. Both the supply and demand sides of the market are important in the determination of equilibrium, when quantity demanded equals quantity supplied. On the demand side, the Law of Demand determines the shape of the demand curve. The determinants of demand then demonstrate how the demand curve shifts. On the supply side, the Law of Supply determines the shape of the supply curve. The determinants of supply then demonstrate how the supply curve shifts. These applications demonstrate when market equilibrium rises or falls.

Chapter 3 on economic efficiency, market failure, and the role of government argues that free markets do not always create desirable outcomes. Markets, for example, may create pollution damage. In addition, markets may underprovide important services, such as public education. The point is that, in the presence of externalities, the market price and quantity may be too high or too low from the perspective of society. This reality provides an economic incentive for government intervention. Other reasons for government intervention include asymmetric information, a lack of market competition, and public goods. Efficient public policies that address these forms of market failure improve society's position; however, inefficient public policy may lead to government failure.

Chapter 4 on elasticity considers the degree of responsiveness of one variable when another variable changes. This chapter provides an additional perspective to the supply and demand model. An example is the price elasticity of demand. When price changes, the question is the extent to which the quantity demanded changes. Given a percentage change in price, the quantity demanded may change by a higher, lower, or the same amount. Many implications of elasticity exist. If consumers are responsive to price changes, they demonstrate elastic responses. If consumers are not responsive to price changes, they demonstrate inelastic responses. Additional applications include cross price elasticity, income elasticity, and elasticity of supply.

Chapter 5 on consumer choice addresses how consumers make decisions in the presence of budget constraints. The determinants of demand establish a framework of analysis by identifying the factors for consumer willingness to pay. The topics of consumer surplus and price discrimination provide additional context. The choice among different forms of output entails a discussion of consumer satisfaction, preferences, and budgets. An application of consumer choice demonstrates that, when making decisions, consumers balance the additional satisfaction from consumption with the cost.

Part II develops the theory of the firm. Chapter 6 examines production, cost, and profit. The objective of the firm is to maximize profit. The production function demonstrates how the firm uses economic resources to produce output. Short-run versus long-run decisions establish whether economic resources are fixed or variable. These timelines provide context for the production decision. In the short run, marginal returns to labor show that additional workers may contribute less to output over time. In the long run, firms may alter all aspects of the production process by changing their operating capacity. The act of producing and selling output leads to revenue generation. With respect to costs, the shape of average and MC curves helps to identify whether a firm is operating at a profit, loss, or break-even position.

Chapter 7 on perfect competition shows that market structure provides context for the theory of the firm. The market structure demonstrates the number of firms in the industry, whether a product is standardized or differentiated, and the degree of difficulty of entry and exit. With perfect competition, a large number of firms exist in the industry, the product is standardized, and it is straightforward for firms to enter and exit the industry. But the result of this market structure is that firms are price takers, taking the price established in the market as a given. In addition, the firm's demand curve is perfectly elastic. For the firm, if the output price exceeds the average total cost (*ATC*), the firm generates a profit. But this outcome provides a signal in the market for other firms to enter. The increase in market supply drives down the price, reducing profit for the typical firm. Price continues to decline until it reaches the minimum point of *ATC*, the break-even point. For the firm, this long-term position creates both allocative and productive efficiency.

Chapter 8 introduces the monopoly market structure, discussing a market in which one firm constitutes the entire industry. The product is standardized, and firms cannot enter or exit the industry. An example is a natural monopoly such as a public utility. Because one firm constitutes the entire industry, the monopoly may sustain a profit over time. However, the monopoly is regulated by the government to make sure it is offering a product in an efficient manner and it is charging a fair price. When the market conditions change, demand may shift or a cost-saving technological advance may occur, which alters the *MC* curve. A monopoly may or may not charge a single price for its output. It may, for example, charge different prices to different customers for reasons other than cost. Price discrimination exists if a monopolist charges a different price to different consumers.

Chapter 9 on oligopoly reviews industries in which a small number of large firms produce a majority of the output. With this market structure, the product is standardized or differentiated. Entrance into and exit out of the industry is difficult. The key is that the firms are strategically interdependent: when making production decisions, they consider the actions of their rivals. Even though the firms are profit maximizers, the oligopoly market arises because of economies of scale. The existence of strategic interdependence means that oligopoly markets are analyzed from a game theory perspective. This perspective establishes rules, strategies, and payoffs. For a firm, a dominant strategy exists when it is the best strategy, regardless of the actions of its rivals. A Nash equilibrium occurs when each player makes the optimal decision.

Chapter 10 on monopolistic competition discusses the market characteristics of a large number of firms, a differentiated product, and easy entry and exit. In the short run, the firms may earn a profit or suffer a loss. In the long run, a movement exists to the break-even point. Monopolistically competitive firms experience a high level of competition. This reality results in product differentiation. An example is non-price competition. Firms may advertise or offer superior service. Because of non-price competition, the ATC curve of firms is higher than it would be otherwise. As a result, the firms do not experience the same level of efficiency as firms in perfect competition.

Part III addresses labor, capital, and financial markets. Chapter 11 on the labor market, an example of a factor market, argues that this market brings together the supply of labor by individuals seeking jobs and the demand for labor by firms wanting to hire. The supply of labor is the time an individual is willing to spend working at different wage rates. The demand for labor is derived from the demand for the goods and services that it helps to produce. Market equilibrium occurs when the market labor supply curve intersects the market labor demand curve, leading to the equilibrium wage and the quantity of labor hired in the market. Several factors cause the market labor supply and market labor demand curves to shift, creating a change in equilibrium price and quantity.

Chapter 12 on capital and financial markets addresses the reality that, with economic decision-making, the question of whether to sacrifice in the present for a payoff in the future occurs on a regular basis. For economic agents, the value in the present of revenue received in the future depends on when the payment is received. In economics, investment occurs when a firm purchases additional units of capital. The financial markets are markets in which money is transferred from economic agents who have excess funds to economic agents who demand the money. Financial markets increase economic efficiency by transmitting money from economic agents who do not have a productive use of it to the economic agents who do. Because of their role in this process of lending and borrowing, financial markets facilitate the process of economic growth.

KEY TERMS

asymmetric information
ceteris paribus
choice

economic resources
efficiency
equity
government failure
government intervention
incentives
industry
labor
land
market economy
market failure
microeconomics
mixed economy
normative analysis
opportunity cost
physical capital
positive analysis
scarcity
trade
tradeoffs

FURTHER READING

Busom, Isabel, Lopez-Mayan, Cristina, and Panades, Judith. 2017. "Students' Persistent Preconceptions and Learning Economic Principles." *The Journal of Economic Education*, 48(2): 74–92.

Gunter, Frank. 2012. "A Simple Model of Entrepreneurship for Principles of Economics Courses." *The Journal of Economic Education*, 43(4): 386–396.

McGoldrick, KimMarie and Garnett, Robert. 2013. "Big Think: A Model for Critical Inquiry in Economics Courses." *The Journal of Economic Education*, 44(4): 389–398.

PART I

MARKETS, CONSUMER CHOICE, AND GOVERNMENT

2

SUPPLY AND DEMAND

MODEL FRAMEWORK

The supply and demand model serves as the most important model in the field of economics. The reason is that it creates a framework to understand how markets operate. As the first chapter explains, a *market* is a mechanism that brings together buyers and sellers for the purpose of exchange. When markets operate efficiently, the price that results from economic activity signals to producers whether to supply more output. But the price also signals to consumers whether to purchase more output. Consider an example.

In California, state and local regulations have made it difficult for developers to build more houses and apartments. During this century, building has occurred, but not enough to satisfy a growing level of demand. The result is higher prices. In certain areas of California, including Los Angeles, San Francisco, and San Jose, housing prices are among the highest in the country. Individuals with higher-paying jobs in technology, management, and other areas buy homes, but many cannot afford the high prices. The supply and demand model demonstrates that, when demand increases and supply is stable, the price increases over time.

As this chapter explains, the supply and demand model provides a framework to consider many economic applications. This is the reason why economists use it to explain market activity. To build the supply and demand model, the chapter discusses markets, the demand side of the market, the supply side of the market, equilibrium, and changes in equilibrium. Along the way, several

DOI: 10.4324/9781003533115-3

applications demonstrate that the supply and demand model serves as a useful method of economic analysis.

MARKETS

The economy exists as a collection of markets. Markets come in all sizes, ranging from farmers markets to stock markets and all markets in between. Although the buyers and sellers may overlap between markets, the collection of traders is normally different in each market, depending on what is bought and sold. Markets for farmers' produce, cell phones, automobiles, or other items exist as output markets. But markets may also include the demand for and supply of economic resources such as labor.

An important part of market analysis is that *aggregation* occurs. Aggregation means the summation of individual market transactions. In the market for cell phones, for example, the question of interest is the number of cell phones that are bought and sold over a specific period of time, such as a year. In the market for t-shirts, it is important to consider how many t-shirts are bought and sold in the industry. Aggregation facilitates this process.

But it is also important to consider the breadth of the market. Economists may study a farmers market in a community, a grocery market in a region, an automobile market in a country, or the cell phone market around the world. The breadth of the market provides the context in which to consider changes in market activity, such as price and quantity. It is also a way to distinguish between microeconomics—the study of economic agents—and macroeconomics, the study of the economy as a whole. In macroeconomics, economists aggregate output at the highest level, bringing together all consumer goods into a category called consumption goods. In microeconomics, economists define markets in a specific context, such as agriculture, electronics, or health care.

Another characteristic of markets is competition. In imperfectly competitive markets, firms have a degree of control over output price. Firms selling athletic shoes may increase or decrease prices when considering market conditions and the actions of their rivals. This possibility also occurs for firms in other market structures, such as airlines, automobiles, and cell phones. But, in perfectly competitive markets, sellers take the market price as a given. In the latter case, the market sets the price, while firms charge this price to customers. In this book, the chapters on market structure analyze the difference between imperfect and perfect competitions.

In markets, when buyers and sellers exchange goods and services for money, they establish their preferences. If buyers are willing and able to buy a specific form of output, they purchase it at the prevailing market price. If they are not interested in buying the output, they do not pay the prevailing price. In both of these circumstances, the decision conveys market information. Output prices provide a signal to producers about the desirability of the products they bring to the market. Prices also establish a framework in which consumers may compare the goods and services they are interested in buying. If they have a choice between several different brands, the price provides a way for consumers to make decisions.

DEMAND

Demand refers to the maximum amount of a good or service that consumers are willing and able to buy at different prices over a specific period of time, ceteris paribus. *Willingness-to-pay*, an important characteristic on the demand side of the market, involves the consumer's valuation of a good or service. If consumers exhibit demand for something, they are willing and able to purchase it. Two issues provide context. First, consumers have different preferences with respect to their willingness-to-pay. Some consumers purchase whole food, but others prefer fast food. Second, consumers may experience a market price that is less than their willingness-to-pay. In this case, they derive value when they purchase products. When consumers make their purchasing decisions, they signal to producers which goods and services to bring to the market.

To establish a market demand curve, it is important to consider that it is the summation, or aggregation, of individual demand curves. For a specific form of output, such as cell phones, one consumer may be willing and able to spend more than another consumer. By aggregating across all consumers of the product, a market demand curve shows how consumers demand output at different prices.

The market demand curve focuses on the *Law of Demand*: as the market price increases, the quantity demanded decreases, ceteris paribus. That is, when consumers have to pay more for a good or service, they will purchase less in a specific time period. The inverse relationship between price and quantity exists because consumers substitute away from more expensive products in order to purchase less expensive products. The market for electronic devices provides an example. When newer and less-expensive products come to the market, consumers buy them, substituting away from more expensive alternatives.

Building a market demand curve requires a *demand schedule*, a table that provides the quantity of a good or service demanded at different prices. In the column on quantity demanded in Table 2.1, the hypothetical data show the annual quantity of cell phones that consumers are willing and able to purchase at different market prices. As the price decreases, consumers are willing and able to purchase more output. For example, at a price of $1,000, consumers demand 10 million units. At a price of $400, consumers demand 40 million units. These different prices and quantities demonstrate the Law of Demand.

Although demand curves reflect individual consumer preferences, economists use market demand curves to forecast changes in price and quantity. It is important to keep in mind, however, that market demand curves may include thousands or millions of consumers (such as with automobile or cell phone industries). For economists, estimating market demand curves requires sophisticated statistical techniques. But for the purpose of this book, the point is that the market demand curve demonstrates the total amount of goods or services that consumers are willing and able to purchase at different prices, holding constant the nonprice determinants. To draw a *demand curve*, graph the numbers in the demand schedule.

Table 2.1 Demand schedule for cell phones

Price ($)	Quantity demanded (millions)
$1,200	0
$1,000	10
$800	20
$600	30
$400	40
$200	50

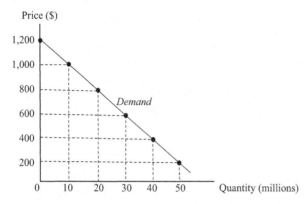

Figure 2.1 Demand for cell phones

In Figure 2.1, the market demand curve slopes downward, demonstrating the inverse relationship between price and quantity. The demand curve is a straight line, but demand curves may be nonlinear and downward-sloping.

Along the demand curve, the price changes. Suppose the price begins at $800 and increases to $1,000 per unit. Because of the Law of Demand, a decrease in quantity demanded occurs from 20 million to 10 million units. In contrast, if the price starts at $400 and decreases to $200, an increase in quantity demanded occurs from 40 million to 50 million units. If the price of a good or service changes, a movement along the demand curve alters the quantity demanded.

SUPPLY

Supply consists of the maximum amount of a good or service that producers are willing and able to sell at different prices over a certain period of time, ceteris paribus. Market supply consists of the summation of the individual supply curves of all firms in an industry. For a specific form of output, firms experience rising opportunity costs when they increase production. One reason is the reality of diminishing returns from the employment of additional economic resources. Another reason is that, when production increases, firms must either employ additional economic resources or have existing workers provide overtime. In either case, the cost of production rises.

As the quantity supplied increases, the cost of providing additional units of output rises. This relationship relates to the *Law of Supply*: as price increases, quantity supplied increases, ceteris paribus. In contrast, as price decreases, suppliers will produce fewer goods or services, all else equal. When the price declines, a lower potential for profit exists.

In the same way that the demand curve demonstrates the Law of Demand, the *supply curve* demonstrates the Law of Supply. The supply curve shows the maximum amount of output that producers bring to the market at different prices. While the demand curve illustrates an inverse relationship between the price and quantity demanded, the supply curve illustrates a direct relationship between the price and quantity supplied. That is, the supply curve slopes upward.

Building a supply curve requires a *supply schedule*, a table that provides the quantity of a good or service supplied at different prices. In the column on the quantity supplied in Table 2.2, hypothetical data show the annual quantity of cell phones that producers are willing and able to sell at different prices. As the price increases, producers are willing and able to supply more output. For example, at a price of $400, producers supply 20 million units. At a price of $1,000, producers supply 50 million units. This is an illustration of the Law of Supply.

To draw a supply curve, graph the numbers in the supply schedule. In Figure 2.2, the market supply curve slopes upward. The supply curve demonstrates the quantity supplied that results from each market price, holding constant the nonprice economic determinants.

Table 2.2 Supply schedule for cell phones

Price ($)	Quantity supplied (millions)
$1,200	60
$1,000	50
$800	40
$600	30
$400	20
$200	10
$0	0

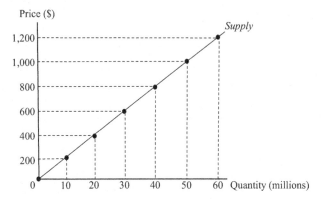

Figure 2.2 Supply of cell phones

Along the supply curve, the price changes. Suppose the price begins at $800 and increases to $1,000 per unit. Because of the Law of Supply, the quantity supplied increases from 40 million to 50 million units. In contrast, if the price begins at $800 and decreases to $600, the quantity supplied decreases from 40 million to 30 million units.

EQUILIBRIUM

When quantity demanded equals quantity supplied, *equilibrium* occurs (point *a* in Figure 2.3). Producers and consumers agree on the equilibrium price ($600) and quantity (30 million). At equilibrium, the market clears.

In a free market, the forces of supply and demand determine the equilibrium price and quantity. No market coordinator exists. In the absence of government controls, prices will gravitate to equilibrium. At a price of $800, the quantity supplied of 40 million units is greater than the quantity demanded of 20 million units. At this price, a *surplus* exists. The market does not clear. At this price, producers want to sell a level of output that is greater than what consumers are willing and able to buy. What is the implication of this imbalance? Producers decrease the price until the market clears at point *a*. At a price of $400, the quantity demanded of 40 million units is greater than the quantity supplied of 20 million

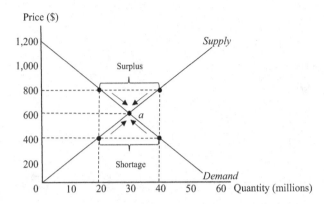

Figure 2.3 Equilibrium price and quantity

units. At this price, a *shortage* exists. The market does not clear. At this price, buyers want to purchase a level of output that is greater than what producers want to sell. In this case, the price rises until it reaches the market-clearing equilibrium at point *a*.

The point is that, if a non-market-clearing position exists, the price mechanism adjusts to eliminate a surplus or shortage. This mechanism is often referred to as the *invisible hand of the market* when buyers and sellers operate in a system of mutual interdependence. But the speed in which the price adjusts depends on the market. In stock, bond, and money markets, the price adjusts quickly as traders buy and sell assets. In labor markets, the price adjusts slowly as buyers and sellers consider their options.

CHANGES IN EQUILIBRIUM

After the establishment of the price and quantity, the economic conditions remain until a nonprice determinant changes. When a change occurs, supply shifts, demand shifts, or they both shift, establishing a new equilibrium condition.

DEMAND SIDE OF THE MARKET

The demand curve shifts with changes in nonprice determinants:

- Tastes and preferences
- Income
- Number of buyers

- Prices of related goods
- Future expectations

If consumer tastes and preferences increase, then consumers are willing and able to buy more output at each price. With a new cell phone, an increase in demand occurs, shifting the demand curve to the right. In contrast, if consumer tastes and preferences decrease, a decrease in demand occurs, shifting the demand curve to the left.

With changes in income, the shift in demand depends on the type of good. When income increases, the demand for *normal goods* increases and the demand curve shifts to the right. Examples of normal goods include electronics, high-end restaurants, and organic food. When income increases, the demand for *inferior goods* decreases and the demand curve shifts to the left. Examples of inferior goods include discount clothing, generic products, and used cars.

In a market, the number of buyers may change. If the number of buyers increases, demand increases, shifting to the right. If the number of buyers decreases, demand decreases, shifting to the left.

The goods and services that consumers buy may be related to other goods and services. *Complements*, such as hot dogs and buns, are consumed together. When the price of hot dogs increases, the demand for buns decreases. *Substitutes*, such as Coca-Cola and Pepsi, are consumed instead of one another. When the price of Coca-Cola increases, the demand for Pepsi increases.

With future expectations, forecasts impact decision-making today. If consumers expect future product shortages and higher future prices, they increase their demand today. If they expect a future sale price, they decrease their demand today.

SUPPLY SIDE OF THE MARKET

The supply curve shifts with changes in nonprice determinants:

- Costs of economic resources
- Production technology
- Number of sellers
- Prices of other forms of output
- Taxes and subsidies
- Future expectations

The cost of economic resources may rise or fall according to market conditions. If the wages of workers increase, all else equal, the cost of production rises for firms for each unit of output. As a result, market supply decreases, shifting to the left. In contrast, if the wages of workers decrease, the cost of production falls. Market supply increases, shifting to the right.

Over time, changes in production technology occur. Technology determines how much output the firms produce given the level of economic resources. An example of an improvement in technology is when firms produce more output per unit of time. In this case, supply increases, shifting to the right.

In a market, the number of sellers may rise or fall. If the number of sellers increases, ceteris paribus, additional firms produce more output, increasing supply and shifting it to the right. If the number of sellers decreases, supply falls, shifting it to the left.

Firms are flexible with the output they produce. Vehicle manufacturers produce cars, trucks, and SUVs. Farmers grow different vegetables. Restaurants sell different types of food. A change in the price of one form of output influences the production of other forms of output. An increase in the price of SUVs encourages automobile manufacturers to produce fewer cars and trucks. An increase in the price of carrots encourages farmers to substitute away from celery. An increase in the price of pizza causes restaurants to sell less pasta.

The government implements taxes and subsidies. Business taxes, which are payments from businesses to the government, increase production costs; however, subsidies, which are payments from the government to businesses, decrease production costs. If business taxes increase, all else equal, production cost rises, decreasing supply and shifting it to the left. If subsidies increase, production costs fall, increasing supply and shifting it to the right.

Future expectations are important on the supply side of the market. If firms think that future prices will be higher than today's prices, they will decrease supply today in anticipation of making more money over time. An example is if home builders forecast higher future home prices. In this case, they decrease supply today. As a result, market supply shifts to the left. In contrast, if firms think that future prices will be lower than today's prices, they increase supply today in anticipation of making more money in the present. Market supply shifts to the right.

SINGLE SHIFTS

With single shifts, a determinant of supply or demand changes. Suppose consumer tastes and preferences increase for cell phones. First, which side of the market is relevant? In this case, a demand-side determinant changes. Second, which way does the demand curve shift? Because an increase in consumer tastes and preferences means that consumers are willing and able to purchase more output at a given price, demand increases and shifts to the right (Figure 2.4). When demand shifts from D_0 to D_1, the equilibrium moves from point a to point b. The equilibrium price increases from \$600 to \$800. Equilibrium quantity increases from 30 million to 40 million units.

The example demonstrates that when demand increases and shifts to the right, both equilibrium price and quantity increase. In contrast, if demand decreases and shifts to the left, both equilibrium price and quantity decrease. To understand the range of scenarios on the demand side, it is important to link changes in the determinants of demand with market outcomes.

Suppose production technology improves. First, does the shift occur on the demand side or supply side of the market? The answer is the supply side. A change in production technology is a supply-side determinant. Second, which way does supply shift? The answer is a rightward shift, which means an increase in supply (Figure 2.5). When supply shifts from S_0 to S_1, equilibrium moves from point

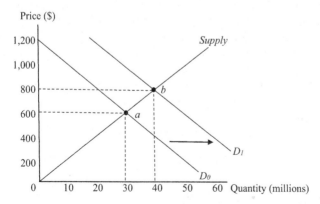

Figure 2.4 Increase in demand

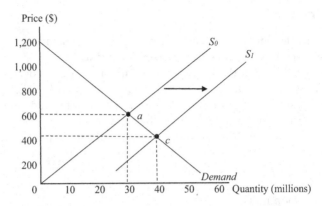

Figure 2.5 Increase in supply

Table 2.3 Single shifts and market outcomes

Shift	Change in price	Change in quantity
Demand increases (shifts to the right)	Increase	Increase
Demand decreases (shifts to the left)	Decrease	Decrease
Supply increases (shifts to the right)	Decrease	Increase
Supply decreases (shifts to the left)	Increase	Decrease

a to point *c*. The equilibrium price decreases from $600 to $400, while the equilibrium quantity increases from 30 million to 40 million units. To summarize, when supply increases and shifts to the right, price decreases and quantity increases. In contrast, when supply decreases and shifts to the left, price increases and quantity decreases.

To understand the range of scenarios on the supply side, it is important to link changes in the determinants of supply discussed earlier with market outcomes. In addition to the previous example of a change in technology, the other determinants are costs of economic resources, number of sellers, prices of other forms of output, taxes and subsidies, and future expectations. For shifts in both supply and demand, Table 2.3 summarizes the market outcomes.

DOUBLE SHIFTS

With double shifts, both supply and demand shift. The key to understanding double shifts is that either the change in price or

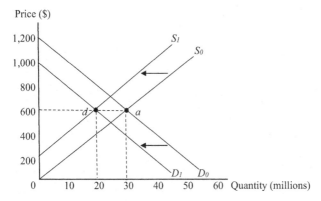

Figure 2.6 Decrease in both supply and demand

the change in quantity is indeterminate. Suppose a normal good and a decrease in income on the demand side and a decrease in the number of sellers on the supply side. In this example, both demand and supply decrease, shifting to the left (Figure 2.6). A movement occurs from point *a* to point *d*. But the example does not specify the magnitude of the shifts. In the figure, demand and supply decrease by the same amount, which leads to a decrease in equilibrium quantity and no change in price. But if demand decreases by a larger magnitude than supply, the price will decrease. In contrast, if demand decreases by a smaller magnitude than supply, the price will increase.

Because all three of these outcomes are possible (increase in price, decrease in price, or no change in price), the change in price is indeterminate. The reader is encouraged to draw the other double shifts to verify the market outcomes in Table 2.4.

Table 2.4 Double shifts and market outcomes

Shift	Change in price	Change in quantity
Demand increases and supply increases	Indeterminate	Increase
Demand decreases and supply decreases	Indeterminate	Decrease
Supply increases and demand decreases	Decrease	Indeterminate
Supply decreases and demand increases	Increase	Indeterminate

KEY TERMS

aggregation
complements
demand
demand curve
demand schedule
equilibrium
inferior goods
Law of Demand
Law of Supply
market
normal goods
perfectly competitive markets
shortage
substitutes
supply
supply curve
supply schedule
surplus
willingness-to-pay

FURTHER READING

Geerling, Wayne, Mateer, G. Dirk, Wooten, Jadrian, and Damodaran, Nikhil. 2023. "ChatGPT Has Aced the Test of Understanding in College Economics: Now What?" *The American Economist*, 68(2): 233–245.

Hong, Bei. 2019. "A Demand and Supply Game Exploring Global Supply Chains." *The Journal of Economic Education*, 51(1): 42–51.

Staples, Aaron, Sackett-Taylor, Hillary, Forgue, Jason, Brewer, Stephanie, and Sarnikar, Supriya. 2020. "A Mixed Methods Approach to Uncover Common Error Patterns in Student Reasoning of Supply and Demand." *The Journal of Economic Education*, 51(3–4): 271–286.

3

ECONOMIC EFFICIENCY, MARKET FAILURE, AND THE ROLE OF GOVERNMENT

MARKETS AND INCENTIVES

The supply of and demand for output create a market price and level of quantity. In the market for cell phones, the price mechanism establishes an incentive for economic resources to flow into this area of production. But the production of cell phones requires three important steps: the extraction of raw materials, manufacture of components, and assembly. Consider each step. The raw materials that go into cell phones include iron, aluminum, copper, lead, zinc, and other materials. To bring these raw materials to market, extraction occurs in countries around the world, including Chile, China, Russia, South Africa, and many others. Once the raw materials are extracted, they are transported to points of assembly for the process of manufacturing. Smartphones include over 200 components, such as batteries, cameras, circuit boards, liquid crystal displays, microphones, and speakers. Many suppliers in countries around the world manufacture components, sending them to assembly plants that are located in China and India.

Why do economic agents participate in the cell phone market? The reason is the market establishes an incentive to earn a profit. Economic agents act in their own interest by providing what the market wants. This action establishes prices for both the economic resources used in production and the output purchased by consumers. The invisible hand of the market ensures that, in a supply

DOI: 10.4324/9781003533115-4

and demand framework, both producers and consumers experience economic benefits.

Markets exist in all sizes, not just the large market for cell phones. Medium and small markets exist in both urban and rural areas. Virtual markets exist on the internet. Markets of all sizes establish prices and quantities while providing incentives for producers to bring output to the market and consumers to purchase goods and services. But markets also create value. On the supply side, producers benefit when the market sets an equilibrium price that is higher than what they are willing and able to charge. On the demand side, consumers benefit when the market sets a price that is lower than what consumers are willing and able to pay.

Economists have tools to measure the value of market activity. While the next section on economic efficiency discusses these tools, the subsequent sections consider applications of the tools in the context of price controls and market failure. Along the way, the chapter addresses the role of government from an economic perspective.

ECONOMIC EFFICIENCY

Suppose a consumer is interested in purchasing a new smartphone. The consumer is willing and able to pay $1,000 for it. But the price is $800, so the consumer benefits from the price differential. The supplier also benefits: it costs $600 to bring the cellphone to the market. When the transaction occurs, both the buyer and seller experience an economic gain.

On the demand side of the market, consumers seek to find the lowest price available for the good or service they want to buy relative to its economic value. This is the reason why consumers compare prices and read reviews. Consumers are looking for a price that is less than their willingness-to-pay, which is their economic value of the good or service. If the price is less than their willingness-to-pay, consumers experience a surplus value from the transaction. This value is called *consumer surplus*, which means the difference between market price and consumer willingness and ability to pay. Economists measure consumer surplus as the shaded area above market price (P_0) and below demand (Figure 3.1).

On the supply side of the market, when producers sell goods and services, they want to receive the highest price possible. But

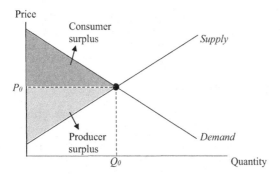

Figure 3.1 Consumer surplus and producer surplus

they also want to sell as many units as possible, given the cost of production, economic resources, and technology. For sellers, this strategy leads to selling output with a reasonable markup (such as cell phones), a high markup (such as rare art), or a low markup (such as t-shirts). In each case, the producers establish a price that is at least equal to their *MC* of production, which is measured along the supply curve. If producers sell for a higher price than the *MC*, they generate *producer surplus*. Economists measure producer surplus as the shaded area below market price (P_0) and above supply (Figure 3.1).

The total economic value generated in a market transaction is equal to the sum of consumer surplus and producer surplus. Along the demand curve, each point serves as the consumer's *MB* from additional units of consumption. The difference between this *MB* and what consumers actually pay is consumer surplus. Along the supply curve, each point serves as the producer's *MC* of bringing additional units of output to the market. The difference between the price the seller receives and the *MC* is producer surplus.

Together, consumer and producer surplus provides the total surplus or total welfare from market transactions. Total welfare is the level of satisfaction for consumers and producers when the market price facilitates exchange. A market producing at equilibrium achieves allocative efficiency. This type of efficiency occurs when economic resources are allocated to their best uses. The results are twofold: the maximization of both consumer and producer surplus and the creation of an economic outcome in which the *MB* of consumption (measured along the demand curve) equals the *MC* of production (measured along the supply curve). But price controls and market failure reduce economic efficiency.

PRICE CONTROLS

When markets operate without government intervention, the equilibrium prices and quantities establish market-clearing positions. Economists characterize these markets as *laissez-faire*, the French term for "let it be." When markets are free, economic resources flow to their most productive uses, consumers purchase the goods and services they want, and producers attempt to earn a profit. Market surpluses and shortages do not persist because price gravitates to equilibrium. Both consumer and producer surpluses are maximized. The problem is that markets may establish efficient outcomes that are not equitable.

A first example is a large urban area that is creating jobs, attracting workers, and experiencing an increase in the cost of housing. If the supply of housing is stable but the demand for housing increases, housing prices rise. In this case, working-class laborers are squeezed out of the housing market, unable to afford higher prices. They may have to move farther away from the business district or relocate to another city. To prevent this from happening, the local government may decide to intervene in the market.

A second example is the wage for entry-level jobs. Because of the rising prices of goods and services and other material aspects of life, many analysts consider the equilibrium wage that exists in the labor market for entry-level jobs as too low. In this case, governments at the state and national levels may implement policies to adjust the wage.

In these examples, the government intervenes in the market by establishing *price controls*, government-mandated maximum or minimum prices for specific forms of output.

PRICE CEILING

In the first example, the rents for apartments in an urban area may not be affordable for members of the working class. In response, the government may implement a housing policy that includes a

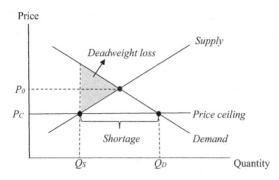

Figure 3.2 Price ceiling

price ceiling on certain apartment units. An effective price ceiling is a maximum price set by the government that is below the equilibrium price (Figure 3.2). For the housing units that qualify, the objective is to prevent the price from reaching equilibrium, because the equilibrium price is too high for lower-income workers.

An example of a price ceiling is the establishment of rent-controlled apartments in New York City after World War II. The policy is still in existence today. Depending on market conditions, the equilibrium price for an apartment in New York City may equal thousands of dollars, too expensive for many working-class individuals. The rent-controlled price for specific apartment units may be set at 1,000 dollars or less. Besides rent control, other contemporary examples of price ceilings include insurance reimbursements, caps on the prices of prescription drugs, and limits on tuition hikes at colleges and universities.

The outcome of this policy is that, at the effective price ceiling (P_C), the market does not clear: quantity demanded (Q_D) is greater than quantity supplied (Q_S), creating a shortage of $Q_D - Q_S$ units. The ceiling price reduces both consumer and producer surplus, creating a *deadweight loss* equal to the shaded area. Deadweight loss is the reduction in efficiency that occurs when the policy moves the market away from the equilibrium position.

To reduce the shortage of affordable housing units, the government could raise the price ceiling toward the equilibrium price. But this would decrease the quantity demanded. In addition, if the price ceiling increases to the equilibrium price or above, it is nonbinding and ineffective. With a ceiling price, the policymakers must balance the increase in equity with the decrease in market efficiency.

PRICE FLOOR

In the second example, the equilibrium wage for entry-level jobs is considered by many analysts to be too low. In the labor market, the supply curve represents the supply of labor by individuals. The demand curve represents the demand for labor by firms. The price of labor is the wage. At the equilibrium wage, entry-level workers are not able to purchase goods and services for a decent standard of living. In response, the government implements a policy that requires a minimum wage for these workers in the form of a *price floor*. An effective price floor (P_F) is a minimum price set by the government, above equilibrium (Figure 3.3). In the United States, a national minimum wage exists, but the states may increase it.

The effective price floor does not create a market-clearing position: at P_F, the quantity supplied is greater than the quantity demanded, creating a surplus of $Q_S - Q_D$ entry-level workers. At the minimum wage, more workers are willing to supply their labor services than the number of jobs that are available. The market conditions, strength of the economy, and preferences for work impact both the supply and demand conditions and the size of the surplus. In theory, the floor price above equilibrium reduces both consumer and producer surplus, creating a deadweight loss equal to the shaded area.

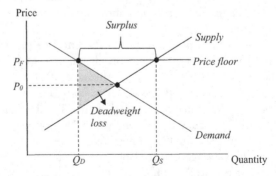

Figure 3.3 Price floor

But empirical research in the field of economics finds that the effect of the minimum wage depends on the level of competitiveness of the labor market. In competitive labor markets, employers do not possess market power over wage decisions. A binding minimum wage has the potential to reduce employment and create involuntary unemployment when individuals want to work but they cannot find jobs. In noncompetitive labor markets, the workers may possess a certain degree of market power. In this case, a minimum wage may lead to gains for the workers as both the supply of and demand for labor curves are steep, reducing the size of the labor surplus at the minimum wage.

MARKET FAILURE AND GOVERNMENT INTERVENTION

Although markets organize the economic behavior of both consumers and producers, they may lead to an inefficient allocation of economic resources. In these cases of market failure, either too much output (overproduction) or too little output (underproduction) occurs. Market failure prevents the price system from establishing an efficient outcome. As a result, the government should intervene to correct the market failure. Four sources of market failure exist: externalities, public goods, asymmetric information, and market power.

EXTERNALITIES

In the presence of an externality, the price that an economic agent pays for a good, service, or economic resource does not equal the price that society pays. An *externality* is the consequence of an economic activity that spills over to third parties that are not involved in the transaction. Externalities create an external cost (negative externality) or external benefit (positive externality).

A negative externality such as pollution from factories leads to an external cost to society. The factories experience the private cost of production, such as rent, wages, and interest payments. But some of the costs spill over to society. The pollution damage serves as an example. The health outcomes associated with air pollution include cancer, cardiovascular disease, neurological disorders, and respiratory disease. The problem is that, in the absence of government intervention, the market does not internalize the external cost of these health problems.

In the graphical form, the supply curve (S_0) represents the marginal private cost (MPC) of production (Figure 3.4). The intersection of S_0 and demand (D_0) establishes the market's equilibrium price (P_M) and quantity (Q_M). But the market equilibrium does not internalize the pollution externality. The social cost of production that pollutes the environment includes both private cost and external cost. Therefore, S_1 includes the marginal social cost (MSC), which entails the MPC to factories and the marginal external cost (MEC) of pollution to society. The vertical distance between points b and a represents the MEC of pollution damage, the additional cost to society from the production of one more unit of output. The shaded area represents deadweight loss. From the perspective of society, the intersection of S_1 and D_0 establishes the optimal point c.

To internalize the negative externality, the government implements a policy that moves the market to the optimal price (P_O), which is higher than the market price (P_M), and the optimal quantity (Q_O), which is lower than the market quantity (Q_M). The higher price and lower quantity lead to less pollution flowing into the environment, better health outcomes, and the internalization of the negative externality.

What government policy would move the market from point a to point c? A common policy is an environmental tax, set equal to the MEC of production. An environmental tax shifts the supply curve

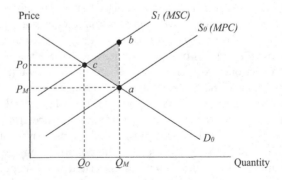

Figure 3.4 Negative externality

from S_0 to S_1, eliminates the deadweight loss, and internalizes the negative externality.

In contrast to the example of a negative externality, a positive externality such as public education generates an external benefit to society. As workers pursue more education and training, they experience higher levels of productivity. Although the individuals that pursue more education and training experience the marginal private benefit (MPB), the economy experiences the marginal external benefit (MEB) of a better-educated workforce.

The problem is that, in the absence of government intervention, the private sector underprovides public education because of the lack of a profit motive. In other words, the private sector does not account for the MEB of education.

In graphical form, the demand curve (D_0) represents the MPB of education (Figure 3.5). The intersection of D_0 and supply (S_0) at point d establishes the market's equilibrium price (P_M) and quantity (Q_M). But the market equilibrium does not internalize the positive externality from public education. The social benefit of education that contributes to society includes both private benefit and external benefit. Therefore, D_1 includes the marginal social benefit (MSB) of education, which entails the MPB flowing to individuals and the MEB flowing to society. The vertical distance between points f and d represents the MEB to society from individuals pursuing more education and training. The shaded area represents deadweight loss. The intersection of D_1 and S_0 at point e establishes the optimal

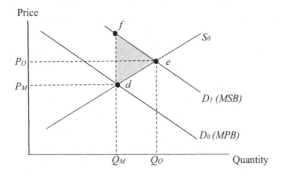

Figure 3.5 Positive externality

position from society's perspective. At point e, the optimal price (P_O) is higher than the market price (P_M), while the optimal quantity (Q_O) is higher than the market quantity (Q_M).

To internalize the positive externality, the government implements a policy that moves the market from point d to point e. At point e, the higher price and quantity lead to more education and training. The government achieves this outcome by providing grants, loans, and subsidies for students of higher education. This policy shifts the demand curve from D_0 to D_1, internalizes the positive externality, eliminates deadweight loss, and provides the incentive for more students to earn college degrees.

PUBLIC GOODS

In private markets, *public goods* such as public parks exist as a source of market failure. The reason that public goods serve as a form of market failure is that they are underproduced in free markets. There is no profit motive involved in the provision of public goods. Therefore, to the extent that society values public goods, the government must provide them.

Public goods are unique because they are both *nonrival* and *nonexclusive* in consumption (Table 3.1). Nonrival means the consumption of one good or service does not decrease the consumption of others. With a public park that lacks congestion, everyone is able to pursue leisure activities. Nonexclusive means that, once a good or service is provided, it is not possible to exclude anyone from its use. A public park that does not have an entrance fee satisfies this characteristic.

With respect to exclusive or nonexclusive activities, an important area of focus is *property rights*, the authority to determine how an economic resource is used. With public goods, the nonexclusive

Table 3.1 Types of goods

| | Property rights | |
Characteristics	Exclusive	Nonexclusive
Rival	Private good	Common good
Nonrival	Club good	Public good

characteristic means that the economic resources used in production are not privately owned. With private goods, the economic resources used in production are privately owned.

If a public good is available, there is little incentive for consumers to pay for it. Economists have found that, with public goods, individuals may serve as *free riders*. Free riders use public goods but do not contribute to their provision. Because of free riders, private firms do not have the incentive to produce goods and services that are nonexclusive and nonrivalrous. As a result, private markets fail to provide the optimal level of public goods, even in situations when society as a whole values their provision.

The optimal provision of public goods differs with respect to theory and reality. In theory, society should provide the level of public goods that equates the market demand for public goods with the market supply. But the total demand for public goods, while reflecting the theoretical willingness-to-pay of individuals, does not mean that the same individuals will actually pay for them (the free rider problem).

In reality, the provision of public goods requires government intervention. Bureaucrats, politicians, special interest groups, and others formulate the quantity of public goods. Because the demand for public goods reflects consumer benefits and the supply of public goods reflects production costs, equating MC and MB yields the optimal quantity. Most people enjoy public parks, but many do not want to pay the taxes necessary for maintenance. As a result of the nonexclusive principle, many individuals do not have the incentive to reveal their true preferences, complicating society's ability to address this form of market failure.

In contrast to public goods, private goods that are provided in the market are both rivalrous and excludable. These are the goods and services that exist in a supply and demand model. One person's consumption of a private good means that others cannot consume it. In addition, a market price means that some consumers cannot afford to purchase it.

In addition to public and private goods, two more categories of goods exist. Common goods such as ocean fisheries or timber in forests are rivalrous in consumption but nonexclusive. The potential problem is overconsumption of common goods, which is called the tragedy of the commons. Because the goods are held collectively, economic agents may race to consume them, leading to depletion.

Club goods such as toll roads and cable television are nonrivalrous in consumption but exclusive. If they are set up in an efficient manner, they do not suffer from congestion. Individuals consuming the goods do not reduce the satisfaction of others who are consuming the goods. But they have prices, so some individuals are excluded from consumption.

ASYMMETRIC INFORMATION

For an efficient market, buyers and sellers must have the same information. If one party has more information than the other, asymmetric information is present. If a real estate agent knows more about a house than a potential buyer, the real estate agent may inflate the price of the house. The presence of an informational imbalance creates prices that do not reflect market value, a form of market failure. Over time, the internet addresses the problem of information asymmetry. When sellers post information online, buyers benefit. In addition, the ability of buyers to post consumer reviews reduces information asymmetries. What is the role of government? The public sector may implement policies that reduce information imbalances, such as consumer protection laws, mandatory disclosure requirements, and licensing procedures. The idea is to make sure that both sides of the market have access to the same information. When this is the case, the price reflects the value of goods and services, while the market establishes an efficient level of output.

MARKET POWER

In the presence of externalities, public goods, or information asymmetries, the market fails to establish an optimal level of output. The problem is an ineffective price signal. The market price does not reflect the MC or MB of an economic activity. But even when the price signal reflects underlying market conditions, the response of economic agents to the price signal may be suboptimal in the presence of *market power*. For firms, market power exists if they are able to set the price above the MC. But market power exists to a certain degree. A small number of large firms that have most of the sales in an industry possess a large degree of market power, but they compete with each other. Monopolies have the most market power because their output constitutes the output of the industry. In the presence of market power, the role of the government is to establish a level playing field. In the case of monopolies, government may make them illegal with the exception of natural monopolies, which exist when the optimal number of firms in a market is one. An example is a public utility. Natural monopolies experience high barriers to entry, so the government regulates the price.

KEY TERMS

consumer surplus
deadweight loss
externality
free riders
laissez-faire
market power
nonexclusive
nonrival
price ceiling
price controls
price floor
producer surplus
property rights
public goods

FURTHER READING

Manning, Alan. 2021. "The Elusive Employment Effect of the Minimum Wage." *Journal of Economic Perspectives*, 35(1): 3–26.
Metcalf, Gabriel. 2018. "Sand Castles Before the Tide? Affordable Housing in Expensive Cities." *Journal of Economic Perspectives*, 32(1): 59–80.

ELASTICITY

PRICE AND ELASTICITY

During the coronavirus pandemic, higher prices bedeviled consumers. More than one year into the crisis, pent-up demand led to more consumer spending. But global supply chain problems persisted. The result of an increase in market demand and a decrease in market supply led to higher prices for many goods. In response, corporate executives assessed the implications of this market outcome. If consumer spending remained strong, higher prices would lead to rising profits. But if consumer spending declined, higher prices would reduce profits. The pattern of consumer behavior had important implications for corporate profits.

Elasticity measures the degree of sensitivity of one variable to a change in another variable. The Law of Demand states that an increase in price leads to a decrease in quantity demanded. But the question for the corporate executives was the extent to which consumers responded to a change in price. If the prices of goods and services increased, to what extent would consumers reduce their expenditure? As a common form of elasticity, the *price elasticity of demand* provides a way to answer the question.

The price elasticity of demand measures the sensitivity of consumers to a change in price. If a small change leads to a large decrease in quantity demanded, consumers are price sensitive. In this case, corporate executives forecast that higher prices will hurt their bottom lines. However, if higher prices lead to small consumer responses, consumers are not price sensitive. When the price rises,

DOI: 10.4324/9781003533115-5

consumers will not reduce their spending by much. The point is that the consumer response to a change in price depends on both the goods in question and market conditions.

When firms increase prices, they consider the price elasticity of demand. Consumer behavior provides information about brand loyalty and market conditions. During the pandemic, consumers adjusted their buying patterns. They turned to the internet for food and retail items. As a result, brick-and-mortar stores were hesitant to increase prices, even to cover rising costs. In addition, consumers decreased their demand for many services, including gyms and movie theaters. Firms offering these services could not increase prices. Many of these firms struggled to stay in business. As this chapter explains, the degree to which consumers respond to a change in price exists as an important concept in the field of economics.

Studying the applications of elasticity on both the demand and supply sides of the market informs economists about consumer and producer behavior. For students, the study of elasticity helps to strengthen problem-solving skills.

ELASTICITY OF DEMAND

On the demand side of the market, the concept of elasticity addresses consumer behavior. For two reasons, this behavior is important to firms. First, it signals how consumers react to a change in price. Second, it reveals how a change in price impacts a firm's total revenue (TR).

PRICE ELASTICITY OF DEMAND

The price elasticity of demand (E_D) measures the responsiveness of quantity demanded to a change in price:

$$E_D = \frac{\text{Percentage change in quantity demanded}}{\text{Percentage change in price}}$$

If the price of cell phones increases by 4 percent and the quantity demanded decreases by 8 percent, the price elasticity of demand is calculated in the following manner:

$$E_D = \frac{-8\%}{4\%} = -2$$

In this case, consumers are responsive to the change in price. But the degree of responsiveness depends on the specific good or service. If the price of gasoline increases by 4 percent and quantity demand decreases by 2 percent, consumers are less responsive to the price change:

$$E_D = \frac{-2\%}{4\%} = -0.5$$

When economists calculate percentage changes, they use the midpoint method. It demonstrates how a percentage change in price from P_0 to P_1 leads to a percentage change in quantity demanded from Q_0 to Q_1. In a movement from point a to b in Figure 4.1, the price increases from \$2 (P_0) to \$3 (P_1). The quantity demanded decreases from 80 (Q_0) to 60 (Q_1).

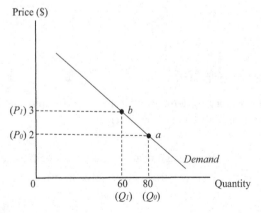

Figure 4.1 Rules of elasticity and total revenue

To calculate the percentage change for quantity demanded with the midpoint formula, plug the quantities into the following equations:

Percentage change in quantity demanded

$$= \frac{Q_1 - Q_0}{\dfrac{(Q_1 + Q_0)}{2}}$$

$$= \frac{60 - 80}{\dfrac{(60 + 80)}{2}} = \frac{-20}{\dfrac{(140)}{2}} = \frac{-20}{70} = \frac{-2}{7}$$

$$= -0.286$$

To calculate the percentage change in price with the midpoint formula, plug the prices into the following equation:

Percentage change in price

$$= \frac{P_1 - P_0}{\dfrac{(P_1 + P_0)}{2}} = \frac{3 - 2}{\dfrac{(3 + 2)}{2}} = \frac{1}{\dfrac{5}{2}} = \frac{2}{5}$$

$$= 0.400$$

To calculate the price elasticity of demand, plug the numbers into the formula for E_D:

$$ED = \frac{\text{Percentage change in quantity demanded}}{\text{Percentage change in price}}$$

$$= -\frac{0.286}{0.400} = -0.715$$

The calculation of the price elasticity of demand yields a negative number. The reason is the Law of Demand: when price increases, quantity demanded decreases. But to simplify the process, economists take the absolute value of E_D. This step turns the negative number into a positive number: $\left| E_D \right| = \left| -0.715 \right| = 0.715$. Using $\left| E_D \right|$, the price elasticity of demand is characterized in the following manner:

- Elastic: $\left| E_D \right| > 1$ (downward-sloping demand curve but flat)
- Inelastic: $\left| E_D \right| < 1$ (downward-sloping demand curve but steep)
- Unit elastic: $\left| E_D \right| = 1$ (downward-sloping demand curve)
- Perfectly elastic: $\left| E_D \right| = \infty$ (horizontal demand curve)
- Perfectly inelastic: $\left| E_D \right| = 0$ (vertical demand curve)

In the above problem, the absolute value of the price elasticity of demand equals 0.715; therefore, the price change occurs in the inelastic range of the demand curve. In this case, the consumer is not sensitive to a change in price.

The characterization of elasticity describes consumer behavior. In the elastic range, consumers are sensitive to price changes. The percentage decrease in quantity demanded is greater than the percentage increase in price. In this situation, if the price of one good increases, consumers switch to substitute goods. In the inelastic range, consumers are not sensitive to price changes. The percentage decrease in quantity demanded is less than the percentage increase in price. In this situation, if the price of one good increases, consumers do not switch to alternative goods. The good in question may be highly desirable or necessary, such as a prescription drug. When the calculation is unit elastic, the percentage decrease in quantity demanded equals the percentage increase in price.

The perfectly elastic and inelastic examples are special cases. With perfectly elastic demand, the smallest increase in price leads to zero units of output sold. This outcome occurs in perfectly competitive markets when firms are price takers. With perfectly inelastic demand, consumers demonstrate no response to a price increase. This possibility exists with a lifesaving drug: the consumer must have it no matter the increase in price.

DETERMINANTS OF THE ELASTICITY OF DEMAND

What determines the elasticity of demand? The four determinants are the good's depiction, proportion of income spent on the good, degree of substitutability, and time period.

With the good's depiction, a *luxury* good is a nonessential purchase that conveys creative expression, superior performance, and other characteristics. Examples include designer clothes and high-end vehicles. Luxury goods are elastic because consumers switch to alternatives when the price increases. In contrast, a *necessity* is an essential purchase. Examples are staple food items, cell phone service, and utilities. When price increases, consumers continue to purchase necessities. As a result, necessities are inelastic.

With the proportion of income spent on a good, households spend a certain percentage of their money on specific goods and services. The smaller the percentage of a household budget spent on a good, the lower the elasticity of demand. For example, some households purchase coffee and tea, but this expenditure represents a small percentage of the budget. An increase in the price of coffee or tea by 20 percent does not alter the households' level of spending in a meaningful way. In contrast, households spend a larger proportion of their budget on housing. This item has a high demand elasticity. If rent increases by 20 percent, household purchasing power declines. The household may have to look for a new place to live.

With the degree of substitutability, a consumer may switch to another good when a price increase occurs. But the harder it is for a consumer to switch, the more inelastic is demand. If a good has few close substitutes, such as gasoline for a combustion engine, the consumer is less sensitive to an increase in price. If a good has many substitutes, such as books, it is easier for consumers to switch to competing items. These latter goods have higher demand elasticities.

With the time period, consumers have a certain amount of time to make decisions. When consumers have little time, demand is inelastic. An example is when the price of gasoline increases in a short period of time. Consumers do not have time to adjust their driving patterns. With more time to adjust, demand elasticity is more elastic. If consumers forecast that gasoline prices will remain high for a long period of time, they may switch to more fuel-efficient vehicles.

For firms, the elasticity of demand serves as a useful calculation. It conveys how consumers respond to a change in price. It also demonstrates how sales adjust. Firms that cannot keep inventory stocked because of strong consumer demand may increase the price without losing customers. Firms with declining customer bases may not feel confident in raising the price. In the latter case, if price increases, the consumers may switch to other products.

ELASTICITY AND TOTAL REVENUE

The calculation of *TR* provides a method to evaluate how a change in price alters a firm's economic position. Total revenue equals the per-unit price of a good or service (*P*) times the number of units sold (*Q*):

$$TR = P \times Q$$

The degree to which the number of units sold responds to a price change impacts *TR*. As the following examples demonstrate, *TR* changes along the demand curve. But the extent to which *TR* changes when the price goes up or down depends on the shape of the demand curve. In Figure 4.2, the demand curve is relatively inelastic (steep). In a movement from point *a* to *b*, consumers display a low degree of sensitivity to a change in price. Price increases from $8 to $12, while quantity demanded decreases from 70 to 60 units of output.

In the movement from *a* to *b*, the smaller shaded rectangle yields a decrease in *TR*: $TR = P \times Q = \$8 \times (70 - 60) = \$80$. The larger shaded rectangle yields the increase in *TR*: $TR = P \times Q = (\$12 - \$8) \times 60 = \$240$. Overall, *TR* increases: $240 - 80 = 160. While the firm loses some customers when the price increases, the remaining customers are willing to pay the higher price. Because

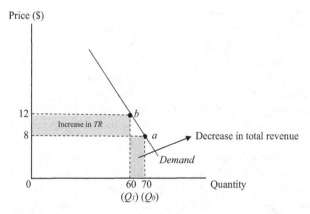

Figure 4.2 Change in total revenue with relatively inelastic demand

the demand curve is relatively inelastic, the firm generates more revenue with a higher price.

In Figure 4.3, the demand curve is relatively elastic (flat). Consumers demonstrate a higher degree of sensitivity to a change in price. With a movement from point a to b, the price increases from $8 to $12. Quantity demanded decreases from 70 to 30 units of output. The larger shaded rectangle yields a decrease in TR: $TR = P \times Q = \$8 \times (70 - 30) = \$320$. The smaller shaded rectangle yields the increase in TR: $TR = P \times Q = (\$12 - \$8) \times 30 = \$120$. Overall, the TR declines: $\$120 - \$320 = -\$200$. When the price increases, many consumers switch to substitute products. Because demand is relatively elastic, the firm loses revenue.

With elasticity and TR, two points are important. First, along a demand curve, TR changes. That is, at different prices and quantities, the calculation of TR yields different results. Second, along the demand curve, elasticity changes. In Figure 4.4, the top graph shows a demand curve. Along the demand curve, elasticity changes when price changes. The bottom graph shows how TR changes when price decreases from $14 to $0.

At different points along the demand curve, it is possible to calculate TR. In the top graph, when the price is $12 and the quantity demanded is 10 units, $TR = \$120$. When the price is $10 and the quantity demanded is 20 units, $TR = \$200$. In the top portion of the demand curve, a decrease in price leads to an increase in TR. This is the elastic portion of the demand curve. In the middle portion of the demand curve, TR remains constant when price changes. For example, when the price is $8 and the quantity

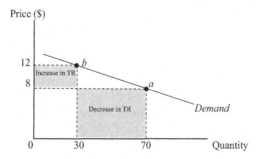

Figure 4.3 Change in total revenue with relatively elastic demand

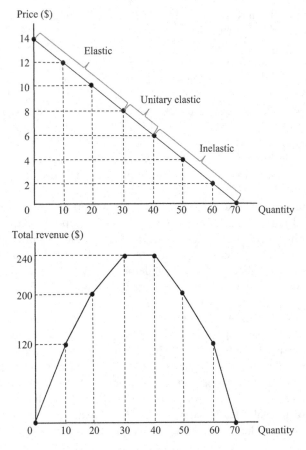

Figure 4.4 Elasticity of demand and total revenue

demanded is 30 units, TR = $240. When the price is $6 and the quantity demanded is 40 units, TR = $240. In the bottom portion of the demand curve, a decrease in price leads to a decrease in TR, signifying the inelastic portion of the demand curve.

These relationships are reflected by the rules of demand, elasticity, and TR (Table 4.1). When price increases, TR decreases in the elastic section of the demand curve but increases in the inelastic section of the demand curve. When price decreases, TR increases in the elastic section of the demand curve but decreases in the inelastic

Table 4.1 Rules of elasticity and total revenue

	Elasticity		
Price change	Elastic	Inelastic	Unit Elastic
Increases	TR decreases	TR increases	TR stays the same
Decreases	TR increases	TR decreases	TR stays the same

section of the demand curve. With unitary elasticity, a change in price yields no change in *TR*.

CROSS PRICE ELASTICITY OF DEMAND

The price of related goods serves as a determinant of demand. The *cross price elasticity of demand* (E_{XY}) acknowledges that some goods are related. This calculation measures the percentage change in the demand for good *X* with a percentage change in the price of good *Y*:

$$E_{XY} = \frac{\text{Percentage change in demand for X}}{\text{Percentage change in the price of Y}}$$

When the price of good *Y* changes, consumers may alter their consumption of good *X*. In calculating the numerical value of E_{XY}, it is important to consider the sign. If E_{XY} is positive, the two goods are substitutes. If E_{XY} is negative, the two goods are complements. If the price of Pepsi (good *Y*) increases by 10 percent and the demand for Coca-Cola (good *X*) increases by 10 percent:

$$E_{XY} = \frac{10\%}{10\%} = 1$$

Coca-Cola and Pepsi are substitutes. When the price of Pepsi rises, some consumers switch to Coca-Cola. As another example, suppose the price of gasoline (good *Y*) increases by 5 percent, but the demand for SUVs (good *X*) decreases by 5 percent:

$$E_{XY} = \frac{-5\%}{5\%} = -1$$

Because the answer is negative, gasoline and SUVs are complements. Individuals consume the products together. When the price
of gasoline rises, the demand for SUVs falls. At a higher price for
gasoline, consumers are less likely to purchase vehicles with large
gasoline tanks.

Cross price elasticity provides information about buyers and sellers. Buyers may purchase goods together or instead of one another.
If two goods are complementary, sellers bundle them together,
encouraging consumers to purchase them at the same time. When
goods are unrelated, $E_{XY} = 0$. In this case, when the price of good
Y changes, the demand for good X does not change.

INCOME ELASTICITY OF DEMAND

Income serves as a determinant of demand. The *income elasticity of
demand* (E_I) measures the percentage change in demand that results
from a percentage change in income:

$$E_I = \frac{\text{Percentage change in demand}}{\text{Percentage change in income}}$$

When income changes, E_I demonstrates the degree of sensitivity
of consumer demand. The calculation of E_I is classified into three
ways. First, if $0 < E_I < 1$, the good is a normal good: an increase
in income leads to an increase in demand. Second, if $E_I > 1$, a luxury exists: additional income increases demand even more. Third,
if $E_I < 0$, an inferior good exists: an increase in income leads to a
decrease in demand. In the latter case, the inferior goods may not
experience a lower quality; however, consumers purchase less when
income rises. It may be the case that some consumers view specific
goods as inferior while others view them as normal. For example,
one consumer may view dining in restaurants as a normal good.
But another consumer may view dining in restaurants as an inferior good, ordering delivery more when income rises. Consumer
behavior is therefore an empirical question and subject to investigation. The different measures of demand elasticity contribute to this
process of identification.

ELASTICITY OF SUPPLY

On the supply side, producers respond to an increase in price by bringing more output to the market. But an important question is the degree to which quantity supplied changes.

Suppliers such as those in the restaurant industry experience highly elastic supply curves. The economic resources needed to produce more output are readily available. When price increases, restaurants employ more workers, use more food inputs, and increase production.

Suppliers in other industries are less responsive to price changes, such as healthcare and housing. The reasons for the inelastic supply include a limited amount of economic resources, a longer time frame for production, and technological constraints. With healthcare, the supply of doctors and nurses is inelastic: these workers require an extensive amount of training for licensing. Labor shortages in the industry lead to higher healthcare costs, longer periods of time for appointments, and less care for those in need. With the housing market, a limited amount of available land in urban areas and strict zoning regulations limit the production of new housing.

The *price elasticity of supply* (E_S) measures the percentage change in quantity supplied divided by a percentage change in price:

$$E_S = \frac{\text{Percentage change in quantity supplied}}{\text{Percentage change in price}}$$

This equation measures movements along the supply curve. If the price increases by 5 percent but the quantity supplied increases by 10 percent, producers are responsive to the change in price. Supply is elastic:

$$E_S = \frac{10\%}{5\%} = 2$$

If the price increases by 5 percent but the quantity supplied increases by 2.5%, producers are less responsive to the change in price. Supply is inelastic:

$$E_S = \frac{2.5\%}{5\%} = 0.5$$

Using E_S, economists characterize the price elasticity of supply in the following manner:

- Elastic: when $E_S > 1$ (upward-sloping supply curve but flat)
- Inelastic: when $E_S < 1$ (upward-sloping supply curve but steep)
- Unit elastic: when $E_S = 1$ (upward-sloping supply curve)
- Perfectly elastic: when $E_S = \infty$ (horizontal supply curve)
- Perfectly inelastic: when $E_S = 0$ (vertical supply curve)

The different degrees of elasticity describe various levels of sensitivity. The factors that determine the price elasticity of supply include the availability of economic resources, the time horizon, market competition, and the availability of substitutes.

When supply is elastic (flat), producers are sensitive to price changes. The percentage increase in quantity supplied is greater than the percentage increase in price. In this case, producers mobilize production when price increases. Economic resources are readily available, firms have longer time horizons and a higher degree of competition, and substitute products exist.

When supply is inelastic (steep), producers are not as sensitive to price changes. The percentage increase in quantity supplied is less than the percentage increase in price. When this occurs, economic resources are not as readily available, firms have shorter time horizons and cannot adjust their productive capacities, a lower degree of competition characterizes the market, and few or no substitute products exist.

The additional characterizations are unitary elasticity and special cases. With unitary elasticity, the percentage change in quantity demanded equals the percentage change in price. With a perfectly elastic supply, the supply curve is horizontal. An example is a special drug that cures a disease. The producer sells it at the highest possible market price, but consumers cannot afford higher prices. With a perfectly inelastic supply, the supply curve is vertical. In cases such as rare art that is fixed in supply, an increase in price leads to no change in the quantity supplied.

ELASTICITY AND TAXATION

Taxes fund government programs such as education, healthcare, and highways. The tax revenue also funds public goods such as fire protection, provides resources for the policies that correct for market failure, and provides the money that flows back into the economy as transfer payments. What is the economic effect of a tax payment? To answer the question, the following discussion addresses the tax rate structure, tax burden, and elasticity. Before addressing these topics, however, it is helpful to understand how the government generates tax revenue:

$$\text{Tax revenue} = \text{Tax rate} \times \text{Tax base}$$

The tax rate is set at a level or percentage of the tax base. An example is a 10 percent tax rate on the value of sales. The tax base is the economic activity subject to the tax, such as income, spending, or wealth. These tax bases are related. They depend on individual decision-making. Individuals control the allocation of their income with respect to spending and saving. The saving helps to determine the level of wealth that accumulates over time.

TAX RATE STRUCTURE

Tax incidence refers to the economic agents who bear the tax burden. The burden depends on the tax rate structure, which establishes the relationship between the tax base and the amount of tax revenue collected during a specific time period. In addressing different tax rate structures, it is important to consider the ratio of taxes paid to the value of the base. The *average tax rate* (*ATR*) equals the dollar value of taxes paid divided by the dollar value of the base:

$$ATR = \frac{\text{Total taxes paid}}{\text{Value of the tax base}}$$

The *marginal tax rate* (*MTR*) equals the additional taxes paid divided by the change in the value of the tax base, where Δ = "change in":

$$MTR = \frac{\Delta \text{Taxes paid}}{\Delta \text{Value of the tax base}}$$

The *ATR* and *MTR* are important for the *proportional tax rate structure*, *progressive tax rate structure*, and *regressive tax rate structure*. A proportional tax rate structure exists when the *ATR* does not change as the tax base changes. A progressive tax rate structure increases the *ATR* when the tax base rises. A regressive tax rate structure decreases the *ATR* when the tax base rises. With the progressive system, individuals make higher tax payments when income rises. With the regressive system, individuals make lower tax payments when income rises.

TAX BURDEN AND ELASTICITY

The tax burden and elasticity address how economic behavior impacts tax policy. An excise tax is regressive, implemented on goods such as gasoline and soda. Lower-income households pay a higher *ATR* than their higher-income counterparts. The tax shifts the supply curve leftward:

- Price increases
- Quantity decreases
- Both consumer surplus and producer surplus decrease
- The government generates tax revenue
- A deadweight loss exists

The economic burden depends on the shape of the demand curve. If demand is elastic and relatively flat, the quantity of output decreases substantially with the implementation of the excise tax because consumers are sensitive to price changes. As a result, sellers bear most of the economic burden. The value of deadweight loss is large. But if demand is inelastic and relatively steep, the decrease in the quantity of output is slight because consumers are willing to pay a higher price. Consumers are not sensitive to price changes. As a result, consumers bear most of the economic burden. The deadweight loss is small.

KEY TERMS

average tax rate
cross price elasticity of demand
elasticity
income elasticity of demand
luxury
marginal tax rate
necessity
price elasticity of demand
price elasticity of supply
progressive tax rate structure
proportional tax rate structure
regressive tax rate structure

FURTHER READING

Allcott, Hunt, Lockwood, Benjamin and Taubinsky, Dmitry. 2019. "Should We Tax Sugar-Sweetened Beverages? An Overview of Theory and Evidence." *Journal of Economic Perspectives*, 33(3): 202–227.

Karaian, Jason and Majerol, Veronica. 2022. "Why Are C.E.O.s Suddenly Obsessed With 'Elasticity'?" *The New York Times*, August 19.

Mendez-Carbajo, Diego. 2017. "Using FRED Data to Teach Price Elasticity of Demand." *The Journal of Economic Education*, 48(3): 176–185.

CONSUMER CHOICE

CHECK OUT

Trips to the grocery store entail numerous choices. Consumers may have a list that guides the decision-making process, but often the variety of products for sale lengthens the trip. Multiple brand names and varieties demonstrate the ability of the economy to bring numerous food and drink items to the marketplace. On a particular trip, a consumer may have a specific amount of money available for expenditure. If this is the case, the consumer must decide what is most important to buy, given the budget and prices of the grocery store items.

Consumer theory is the area of microeconomics that addresses how individuals decide to spend their money based on budget constraints and preferences. The consumer in the example may experience a high level of *utility* (satisfaction from consumption) when purchasing items such as baked goods and prepared foods, but these items may be relatively more expensive than purchasing the cooking ingredients and making the food from scratch. As a result, the consumer must decide whether to buy a fewer number of expensive food items and consume them after arriving home or consume a larger number of inexpensive ingredients that require preparation and cooking.

This decision-making process relates to consumption choices and consumer satisfaction. To address these topics, the chapter discusses the budget, utility, consumer choice, and behavioral economics. The chapter argues that the optimal level of consumption requires a balance between the additional satisfaction from consumption and

DOI: 10.4324/9781003533115-6

per-unit price. But to purchase items at stores or online, individuals must have the willingness and ability to pay. As a result, tastes and preferences are as important for consumer choice as are income and prices.

THE BUDGET

The *budget line* demonstrates the combinations of two goods that an individual may purchase, given income and prices (Figure 5.1). Suppose a college student has $40 per week to spend on food and entertainment. The student buys sandwiches at $8 each and watches streaming programs at $4 each. The programs are purchased in units of two.

The student chooses between different consumption bundles. If the student spends all of the money on sandwiches, the student buys five sandwiches and no programs (bundle *a*). On the budget line, this bundle provides the vertical axis intercept. If the student spends all of the money on programs, the student watches 10 programs and consumes zero sandwiches (bundle *f*). On the budget line, this bundle provides the horizontal axis intercept. But the student may consume the bundles in between. For example, the student may consume four sandwiches by spending $32 on sandwiches at $8 each and watch two programs by spending $8 on programs at $4 each (bundle *b*). Table 5.1 lists the other consumption bundles on the budget line.

With each consumption bundle, the student spends all of the weekly income. As a result, the consumption bundles are characterized

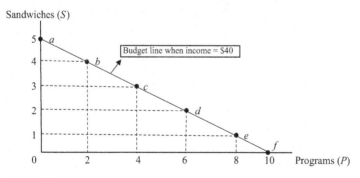

Figure 5.1 Budget line

Table 5.1 Consumption bundles on the budget line

Bundle	Sandwiches	Spending on S ($)	Programs	Spending on P ($)	Total spending ($)
a	5	40	0	0	40
b	4	32	2	8	40
c	3	24	4	16	40
d	2	16	6	24	40
e	1	8	8	32	40
f	0	0	10	40	40

by the *budget constraint*, the total amount of goods and services a consumer may purchase with the budget. In this example, it is expressed in terms of income (M) and the prices of sandwiches (P_S) and programs (P_P):

$$M = P_S S + P_P P$$

For example, plugging into the budget constraint for bundle c yields

$$\$40 = (\$8)(3) + (\$4)(4)$$
$$\$40 = \$40$$

The slope of the budget line includes a minus sign because the line slopes downward. The slope is expressed in terms of intercepts or the *relative price* (P_P/P_S):

$$\text{Slope of the budget line} = -\frac{\text{Vertical intercept}}{\text{Horizontal intercept}} = -\frac{P_P}{P_S}$$

The relative price of programs in terms of sandwiches is the rate at which a program trades for sandwiches. It is the price that the student has to pay—in terms of sandwiches—when the student buys one more program.

UTILITY

The budget line demonstrates the consumption bundles. But the budget line does not show which bundle the individual will choose. This decision requires the consideration of tastes and preferences. How much satisfaction does the student derive from the consumption of sandwiches and streaming programs? When making decisions at the margin, the student decides the next unit of output to buy, considering the price of each item. The student weighs the satisfaction from an additional unit of consumption against the per-unit price.

Utility measures satisfaction. *Total utility* (*TU*) is the level of satisfaction derived from the consumption of goods and services. The objective of the consumer is to maximize *TU* subject to the budget constraint. But, in order to achieve the objective, the individual focuses on *marginal utility (MU)*, the satisfaction derived from an additional unit of consumption (Table 5.2). *MU* is the change in *TU* divided by the change in quantity (*Q*):

$$MU = \frac{\Delta TU}{\Delta Q}$$

The student enjoys the first sandwich more than the first program: the *MU* of the first sandwich is 56 utils, but the *MU* of the first program is 40 utils. For sandwiches, the *TU* from consuming the first unit equals 56 utils, so the *MU* of the first unit is

Table 5.2 Total utility and marginal utility

Quantity of sandwiches (S)	TU_S	MU_S	Quantity of programs (P)	TU_P	MU_P
0	0	0	0	0	0
1	56	56	2	80	40
2	104	48	4	144	32
3	144	40	6	192	24
4	176	32	8	224	16
5	200	24	10	240	8

calculated in the following manner: $MU = \dfrac{\Delta TU}{\Delta Q} = \dfrac{56}{1} = 56$. For programs, the TU from consuming the first two programs equals 80 utils, so the MU per program is calculated in the following manner: $MU = \dfrac{\Delta TU}{\Delta Q} = \dfrac{80}{2} = 40$. The calculation of the other values proceeds in the same manner.

DECREASING MARGINAL UTILITY

As consumption increases, individuals normally experience a lower level of satisfaction on a per-unit basis. Why does this pattern occur? No matter the tastes and preferences, individuals eventually become sated with additional units of consumption. That is, additional units of consumption provide a declining level of utility. The student in the example may enjoy the first sandwich a lot, but experience a lower level of satisfaction from the second sandwich, and an even lower level of satisfaction from the third, and so forth. This principle is known as the *law of diminishing marginal utility*. This law means that, as additional consumption occurs, the rate at which satisfaction increases eventually goes down. With additional units of consumption, it is even possible for MU to reach zero or become negative. When MU equals zero, an additional unit of consumption does not increase the total level of satisfaction. When MU is negative, an additional unit of consumption decreases TU. A rational individual would stop consuming before MU becomes negative.

OPTIMAL LEVEL OF CONSUMPTION

Given the income and prices, how many sandwiches and programs will the student choose? That is, what is the optimal level of consumption? To answer the question, consider both MU and price. As a reminder, the consumer wants to maximize TU subject to the budget constraint. The consumer chooses the consumption bundle that provides the highest level of satisfaction, given the money available to spend.

The problem requires the analysis of MU per dollar spent, the latter determined by the per-unit price: MU/P. In the example, the analysis of MU/P makes it possible to evaluate the consumption choice across both items. Table 5.3 demonstrates how the consumer

Table 5.3 Total utility and marginal utility per dollar

(1) Quantity of sandwiches	(2) TU_S	(3) MU_S	(4) MU_S/P_S	(5) Quantity of programs	(6) TU_P	(7) MU_P	(8) MU_P/P_P
0	0	0	0	0	0	0	0
1	56	56	7	2	80	40	10
2	104	48	6	4	144	32	8
3	144	40	5	6	192	24	6
4	176	32	4	8	224	16	4
5	200	24	3	10	240	8	2

thinks at the margin, making the next decision. At the beginning of the week, the student must decide whether to purchase the first sandwich or the first two programs. Because the student has $40 to spend, the student evaluates how much additional satisfaction is derived per dollar spent, choosing the higher number. In Table 5.3, this information appears in columns four and eight.

Each choice leads to a different MU/P. For example, the first sandwich leads to 7 utils of satisfaction per dollar spent. The first two programs lead to 10 utils per dollar spent. The student chooses the programs, spending $8 in the process. The student must then choose between the first sandwich (7 utils per dollar spent) or the third and fourth programs (8 utils per dollar spent). Again, the student chooses the programs. Now the student has spent $16. The process continues until the student spends the entire weekly budget of $40 (Table 5.4). If the MP/P is identical for two choices, the individual may choose them in either order. An example is the choice between the second sandwich and the fifth and sixth programs.

By following this process, the student spends $16 on two sandwiches (104 utils) and $24 on six programs (192 utils), generating 296 utils of satisfaction. Given the budget constraint, no other combination of sandwiches and programs creates a higher level of satisfaction. This is the reason why the incremental process of decision-making leads to an optimal result.

With the last unit of consumption for both sandwiches and programs, $MU/P = 6$. This result is not a coincidence. The idea is that if one choice leads to a higher level of additional satisfaction

Table 5.4 Optimal choices with a budget of $40

Number	Choice	MU/P	Additional spending ($)	Total spending ($)
1	Consume programs 1 and 2	10	$8	$8
2	Consume programs 3 and 4	8	$8	$16
3	Consume sandwich 1	7	$8	$24
4	Consume sandwich 2	6	$8	$32
5	Consume programs 5 and 6	6	$8	$40

per dollar spent, the individual will make that choice. The *utility maximizing rule* that follows from this observation is:

$$\frac{MU_S}{P_S} = \frac{MU_P}{P_P}$$

The application of the utility maximizing rule is that, for goods (a, b,... n), the consumer will choose the item that provides the highest level of additional satisfaction per dollar spent until MU/P is equalized

$$\frac{MU_a}{P_a} = \frac{MU_b}{P_b} = \cdots = \frac{MU_n}{P_n}$$

DERIVING THE DEMAND CURVE

In the example, the consumer makes an optimal choice by choosing the item with the highest MU per dollar spent. With sandwiches costing $8 each and streaming programs costing $4 each, the consumer purchases two sandwiches and six programs. What would happen with a change in price? The answer is a different consumption bundle. Suppose the price of streaming programs increases from $4 per program to $5 per program. In this case, the student will substitute away from the consumption of programs because they are more expensive. When price increases, the quantity demanded decreases, corresponding to the Law of Demand (Figure 5.2). If the

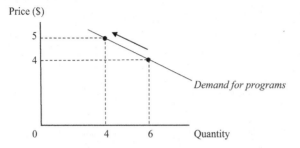

Figure 5.2 Demand for programs

budget remains constant at $40 but the price of programs increases from $4 to $5, the student reduces the consumption of programs from six to four (the student also increases the consumption of sandwiches from two to three).

CHANGE IN INCOME

In addition to a change in price, a change in income alters the consumption bundle. Suppose the original prices of $8 per sandwich and $4 per program. If income increases to $64 per week, the budget line shifts (Figure 5.3). At first, the student could choose between the original consumption bundles, $40 in income, and the original budget line. Now, the student chooses between different consumption bundles, $64 in income, and the new budget line.

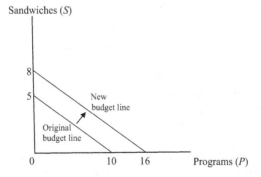

Figure 5.3 Change in income shifts the budget line

Table 5.5 Optimal choices with a budget of $64

Number	Choice	MU/P	Additional spending ($)	Total spending ($)
1	Consume programs 1 and 2	10	$8	$8
2	Consume programs 3 and 4	8	$8	$16
3	Consume sandwich 1	7	$8	$24
4	Consume sandwich 2	6	$8	$32
5	Consume programs 5 and 6	6	$8	$40
6	Consume sandwich 3	5	$8	$48
7	Consume sandwich 4	4	$8	$56
8	Consume programs 7 and 8	4	$8	$64

By using the information in Table 5.3, it is possible to demonstrate how the consumer thinks at the margin. The results are shown in Table 5.5. With respect to the original budget of $40, the first five choices with a budget of $64 are the same. But with more money to spend the student is able to consume the third and fourth sandwiches and seventh and eighth programs. The final consumption bundle of four sandwiches and eight programs increases the student's utility from 296 utils to 400 utils, representing a higher level of satisfaction.

BEHAVIORAL ECONOMICS

MU analysis explains the process of optimal consumer choice, given the budget constraint and prices. This framework is useful in many contexts. But it has limitations.

First, the degree of difficulty is high in solving the problem of consumer choice with *MU* analysis. Individuals may not engage in optimal decision-making. They may be influenced by factors outside of the model framework.

Second, *MU* analysis assumes that individuals have the ability to measure their additional satisfaction from the consumption of more goods or services. Yet, this is a difficult process, even with products such as sandwiches and streaming programs. This reality, however, does not imply that the framework is not useful. It means that the model is limited by the requirement of identifying MU. It is important to note that MU analysis remains the benchmark for most applications of consumer theory in economics.

Third, the analysis requires the calculation of MU divided by price, which may not occur in reality. Nevertheless, consumers often consider whether the additional satisfaction they derive from consumption is worth the price. This is why consumers sometimes choose to purchase an item with a lower level of satisfaction when compared to other options. Even though the item provides a lower level of satisfaction, it has a lower price.

Finally, MU analysis assumes that consumers make rational decisions. In other words, the consumers compare the MB of the next unit of consumption with the MC. But does this method of decision-making occur? Do consumers always make rational choices? A lot of research by economists over the last several decades demonstrates that consumers often behave in irrational ways, making choices without considering the MBs and costs. This is the subject of *behavioral economics*, a method of analysis that uses insights from psychology to explain the decision-making process in economics.

FUNDAMENTALS OF BEHAVIORAL ECONOMICS

In many situations, individuals do not consider the benefits and costs of their actions. This behavior is part of human nature. But the behavior may not be random. It may be predictable. As a result, behavioral economics addresses irrational human behavior that occurs in predictable ways. Because of the irrational nature of some decisions, behavioral economics differs from the standard economic theory posited by MU analysis. It also means that sellers may take advantage of the irrational behavior of buyers.

Behavioral economics establishes a framework of analysis that acknowledges the potential for irrational decision-making. This framework offers three areas of focus. First, behavioral economics provides policy tools that influence behavior. If individuals respond to incentives in multiple ways, dynamic policy tools may account for this reality. Consumers may alter their choices for reasons other than a change in income or relative price. Second, in specific contexts, behavioral economics may yield better predictions of human behavior. Inertia, for example, may serve as the reason why an individual may not make a rational choice. Third, behavioral economics generates new outcomes with human welfare. Problems such as myopia or inattention create differences between the forecasted MU from a potential choice and the actual MU from an action. Accounting for these deviations away from the traditional model of rational choice provides a greater understanding of human behavior.

FORMS OF SYSTEMATIC BIAS

The idea of behavioral economics is that individuals sometimes fail to act according to predictions of the standard economic model of consumer choice. The reason is the standard model assumes that individuals maximize utility subject to a budget constraint. They make rational choices with their consumption decisions. But what if human behavior does not always correspond with model predictions? The implication is that humans do not always weigh the MB against the MC of their actions. A *systematic bias* creates a methodological deviation from an actual decision. Behavioral economics addresses five forms of systematic bias: altruism, framing, overconfidence, problems of self-control, and sunk costs.

With altruism, individuals act out of generosity or goodwill. They think about the needs of others. Donating money to a charity, helping a person with directions, or sharing resources may serve as helpful gestures that do not provide a personal reward besides a positive feeling. But these actions come with a cost in terms of effort, money, or time. Altruism is therefore undertaken as an intentional act, but it does not fit well within the rational model of consumer choice. The rational model assumes that individuals act in their own self-interest. Because altruistic behavior exists as a non-maximizing act of selflessness—individuals helping others during a pandemic or parents sacrificing for their children—the standard economic model struggles to account for it. But economists have included altruistic behavior in some forms of economic analysis, identifying warm-glow altruism. This concept means the individual derives satisfaction when acting in the interest of other people. But this method still raises the problem that helping others does not correspond to the behavior of a self-interested economic agent. Because altruism exists as an important concept, regardless of the outcome of the action, behavioral economists acknowledge the importance of the act.

A second source of systematic bias occurs when individuals make irrational decisions depending on how a product is presented. Framing occurs when individuals make consumption decisions based on how a product is framed, but not on the economic facts of the decision. It is considered a cognitive shortcoming to decide based on the presentation of the product and not the reality of MCs and MBs. For example, stores may offer a deal to "buy one and get one at half price." For consumers, this offer is considered more appealing than the store selling the two products at "25 percent off," even though the cost is the same. As another example, a common selling strategy in the retail sector is to reduce the price of a product by a very small amount in order to appeal to consumers, such as reducing the price from \$10.00 to \$9.99. The difference is one-tenth of one percent, but consumers often find the latter price more appealing. The ability of sellers to influence consumer behavior through the presentation of selling options exists as a framing bias. The idea is that a different presentation of the product encourages consumers to alter their behavior. Another example of framing bias is when sellers convince buyers that they purchase more value than what they pay. Some stores offer products in a continuous sale, even though marking the items down by the same amount establishes the same selling price. When a sale exists, consumers are more inclined to purchase the product. To take advantage of consumers, the stores artificially raise the price of the product and then offer it for sale, anchoring in the minds of the consumers that the product is worth the inflated price.

A third source of systematic bias is overconfidence. For individuals, this feeling may serve as a factor in making successful decisions. But overconfidence may lead to problems. Sellers may take advantage of the tendency, because individuals may believe their judgment is better than it actually is. For example, individuals may think that future outcomes are more likely to happen than they actually are. As a result, they may make mistakes. If an individual forecasts an increase in a stock price, the individual may decide to buy the stock today. But for the transaction to occur, someone else must be willing to sell, forecasting that the stock price will fall. Who is right?

If the individual experiences overconfidence and does not evaluate all of the financial market conditions, the decision to buy may be impulsive. If an online brokerage gives the individual an opportunity to impulsively buy stocks, the online brokerage may take advantage of the individual's overconfidence, especially if the brokerage charges fees for every transaction. As another example, gyms often require long-term contracts. The idea is to lock in regular payments over a certain period of time, such as monthly payments for a year. While an individual may feel confident that they will commit to a regular exercise schedule, in reality, this routine may be difficult to maintain. Diminishing *MU* from additional exercise may discourage the individual from regular trips to the gym. But the gym locks in the monthly payments, regardless of the amount of time spent exercising.

A fourth area of systematic bias is self-control. Individuals may struggle to plan for the future. They may place a higher value on current consumption than on future consumption. The money that individuals save today earns interest, which increases the value of the savings over time. However, even though this process increases the value of money, it means giving up some present consumption. Even though different time preferences are not necessarily irrational, because economic conditions may change in the future, they may distort the process of rational decision-making. Economists refer to this problem in terms of *hyperbolic discounting*, when individuals value immediate payoffs more than future payoffs, even when the latter payoff is greater. With this tendency, individuals may be reluctant to fund retirement programs, even if the employer provides a lucrative matching program. In the present, the contribution to the program decreases the individual's level of disposable income, which reduces current consumption. The problem that hyperbolic discounting introduces in economic models is that individuals may not exhibit time-consistent behavior. Individuals may declare their interests, but when future periods arrive they change their behavior. That is, what individuals think they will do and what they actually do may not be the same. The presence of time-inconsistent behavior complicates the analysis of human decision-making. The problem is that sellers may take advantage of this reality. Credit card companies, for example, may offer low or zero interest rates for the first few months, thus encouraging the consumer to maintain a credit card balance. But the cost of keeping the balance may increase over time.

A final area of systematic bias relates to sunk costs. A sunk cost is money that has already been spent and cannot be recovered. A *sunk cost fallacy* exists if individuals hesitate to cancel an activity because they have invested money in it, even though the abandonment of the activity is a better strategy. A common example is the purchase of a ticket before a concert, theater event, or game. If another activity emerges at the same time and becomes more important, such as preparing for an exam, an individual may hesitate to change plans because they have already paid for a ticket. Economic theory, however, demonstrates that the individual should choose the activity with the highest net benefit, even in the presence of a sunk cost. The decision to change activities should not be based on past payments, but on how the decision impacts an individual's well-being. No matter the choice, the money for the ticket is gone. The sunk cost fallacy often exists when individuals feel they have invested a lot of time or money into an activity. In the market, ticket agencies will leave the losses from the sunk costs with the buyers, reaping the gains. While the idea of making plans ahead of time exists as a prudent strategy, refusing to change plans because of sunk costs leads to irrational decision-making.

KEY TERMS

behavioral economics
budget constraint
budget line
consumer theory
hyperbolic discounting
marginal utility
relative price
sunk cost fallacy
systematic bias
total utility
utility
utility maximizing rule

FURTHER READING

Chetty, Raj. 2015. "Behavioral Economics and Public Policy: A Pragmatic Perspective." *American Economic Review*, 105(5): 1–33.

Gandullia, Luca, Lezzi, Emanuela, Parciasepe, Paolo and Siri, Lidia. 2021. "Altruism and Structure of Values: An Experimental Investigation." *Journal of Interdisciplinary Economics*, 33(1): 103–129.

Hamilton, Rebecca, Mittal, Chiraag, Shah, Anuj, Thompson, Debora and Griskevicius, Vladas. 2019. "How Financial Constraints Influence Consumer Behavior: An Integrative Framework." *Journal of Consumer Psychology*, 29(2): 285–305.

PART II

THEORY OF THE FIRM

6

PRODUCTION, COST, AND PROFIT

ECONOMIC ACTIVITY

Firms are institutions that employ economic resources to produce goods and services. They come in all sizes. A small firm such as a *sole proprietorship* is owned by individuals who are responsible for market decisions and legal outcomes. Small firms undertake numerous forms of economic activity, including construction, real estate, and insurance. Small firms provide the opportunity for entrepreneurs to bring new ideas to the marketplace. A *partnership* is larger. It is an economic arrangement in which two or more people share ownership and manage business operations, sharing in the firm's profits. The examples of partnerships are numerous, including accounting, architecture, and the legal sector. As the largest form of business organization, the *corporation* is incorporated by a group of shareholders. Corporations have investor ownership, legal liability, management under a board of trustees, and markets that often span the globe.

The firm's size, economic resources, and output influence its production decisions. A sole proprietorship that supplies cookies to its customers may experience a surge in demand during the holidays. It hires seasonal workers, impacting its production cost but also its potential for revenue generation. A partnership that focuses on architectural design may establish contracts with city governments. When the economy is growing and tax revenue is flowing into government coffers, the firm receives more business. A corporation that operates on a global scale, producing output for markets around the world, is subject to changing supply and demand conditions,

DOI: 10.4324/9781003533115-8

foreign competition, and public policy. The point is that firms in different industries establish the most efficient way to employ economic resources.

The objective of all firms is to maximize profit. Profit equals *TR* minus *TC*. Consider a vehicle manufacturer that operates on a global scale. The manufacturer purchases parts from all over the world, produces output in several countries, and sells its vehicles in Asia, Europe, and North America. Because of a growing level of demand, rising concerns about climate change, and public policy that encourages production, an incentive exists for the manufacturer to expand the production of electric and hybrid vehicles.

In order to make the production decision, the firm evaluates market conditions, global supply chains, and consumer preferences. Technological advances in the production of key parts, including batteries and electric motors, reduce the cost of production. But challenges remain. For manufacturers that operate in developed countries, the cost of production is higher than for manufacturers that operate in developing countries. Manufacturers operating in China and India, for example, experience lower labor costs than manufacturers in the United States. The former countries establish the appropriate economic infrastructure, including the provision of economic resources, distributional efficiencies, and government subsidies. When a foreign corporation supplies a vehicle in the market at a lower price than its rivals, it has a chance to increase profit, expand market share, and enhance its brand. In response, domestic manufacturers increase productivity and implement new forms of technology.

To analyze the theory of the firm, this chapter addresses production, cost, and profit. While markets differ with respect to their supply and demand conditions, the firms must decide how to employ economic resources in the most productive manner.

PRODUCTION

To maximize profit, the firm decides what to produce, the quantity of output to bring to the market, how to produce, how to acquire economic resources, the payment for its economic resources, and what price to charge. This chapter and the following chapters on market structure demonstrate how the firm addresses these issues.

With each decision, however, the firm does not have an unlimited amount of money to allocate to additional workers. Its market share limits the ability to reach consumers. The objective of profit maximization implies cost minimization, so the firm must consider the cost of its economic resources. Many other challenges exist, including constraints, efficiency, the decision time frame, and output.

CONSTRAINTS

Three constraints limit the economic profit of firms: the information constraint, market constraint, and technology constraint. First, with the information constraint, the firm is limited by the fact that it does not know how the market will change, whether worker productivity will increase over time, if different consumer preferences will impact the demand for output, and the decisions of competitors. To address these uncertainties, firms forecast future market conditions, track worker productivity, evaluate consumer behavior, and analyze the other suppliers in the market. Second, the market constraint refers to the firm's ability to sell output at different prices. This condition depends on the willingness and ability of consumers to purchase goods and services. To influence this factor, firms allocate resources for marketing and advertising, attempting to boost sales, market share, and brand loyalty. Third, in the field of economics, *technology* refers to the method by which a firm turns economic resources into output. Technology includes the responsibilities of workers, the organization of the firm, the layout of the production space, and the capabilities of physical capital. Producing more output requires the employment of additional economic resources, which increases cost and alters profit conditions.

EFFICIENCY

In economics, efficiency refers to the use of economic resources in the most productive way. A firm is operating efficiently if it optimally employs economic resources to maximize the production of output. The achievement of efficiency gains from scarce economic resources serves as an important goal. In economics, two types of efficiency relate to production. *Allocative efficiency* occurs when firms are producing the goods and services that consumers want.

Competitive markets determine this outcome through the forces of supply and demand. When firms allocate economic resources to the production of the output that consumers most desire, the right mix of goods and services is produced. Examples include the production of smartphones instead of flip phones or digital music instead of compact discs. *Productive efficiency* occurs when firms produce goods and services at the lowest cost. With this condition, firms produce the maximum amount of output, given the level of economic resources. Firms use the best available production technology and economic resources to minimize the cost of production. The degree of competition in the market, the economic power of the firm, and production decisions influence whether firms satisfy these efficiency conditions.

DECISION TIME FRAME

Firms decide how much output to produce and what prices to charge. Because the supply and demand conditions change, firms adjust their production decisions. When consumers increase their tastes and preferences for products, firms allocate economic resources to satisfy demand. When more suppliers enter the industry, firms evaluate their production processes to make sure that they are making efficient choices. These decisions are important because they contribute to the economic viability of firms. Correctly forecasting market trends contributes to profit. Making the wrong decision about the use of labor or capital contributes to losses.

The point is that economic decisions have important consequences. But the actions of firms to adjust output and prices depend on the decision time frame. A firm that wants to alter its production in the next few weeks has fewer options than a firm that wants to alter its production in the next few years. In this context, economists identify two time frames.

The *short run* is the period of time in which at least one economic resource is fixed. In the short run, firms cannot alter their plant capacity. But they may alter the variable economic resources, which are the labor or materials that they employ in the production process. If the firms in a specific industry expect a surge in demand over the holiday season, they hire more workers. This flexibility allows the firms to adjust to changing market conditions. But economists do not equate the time frame with a certain number of weeks or months. The short-run means that firms adjust their variable economic resources but not their fixed economic resources.

The *long run* is the period of time in which all economic resources are variable. In the long run, firms may alter their plant capacity. Firms may enter or exit the industry. If firms believe that higher consumer incomes will translate into greater sales over time, they may decide to expand their productive capacities, increase the size of their plants, and ramp up production. But in the long run, if the typical firm is experiencing a profit and it's possible for more firms to enter the industry, additional businesses will join the market, adding to the level of competition. Alternatively, if the typical firm is suffering a loss in competitive markets, businesses will exit.

PRODUCTION IN THE SHORT RUN

Before consumption occurs, goods are produced. Production is the act of turning economic resource inputs into output. But different forms of production occur. Some firms produce final goods and services that are purchased by consumers. Other firms produce intermediate goods that are used in different production processes. Firms in different industries undertake production with numerous economic processes. A baker who turns food inputs into bread implements a much different economic process than a firm that turns materials into cell phones.

But these and other producers employ a *production function*, which demonstrates the amount of output a firm may produce with different combinations of economic resource inputs. For example, the production of output is a function of land, labor, capital, and entrepreneurial ability, the economic resources necessary to produce output. Other inputs include materials and energy. The baker needs flour, salt, water, and other ingredients. The cell phone manufacturer needs the parts that go into cell phones, including batteries, cameras, and speakers. Because firms attempt to maximize profit, they also attempt to minimize cost.

Suppose a bread-baking business is established by an entrepreneur. To simplify the analysis, the production of output (Q) is a function of labor (L) and physical capital (K): $Q = f(L, \bar{K})$. Assume that the physical capital is fixed. To bake bread, the baker uses a

Table 6.1 Total product, marginal product, and average product

Labor	Total product (Q)	Marginal product of labor (MPL)	Average product of labor (APL)
0	0	–	–
1	10	10	10
2	22	12	11
3	30	8	10
4	35	5	8.75
5	38	3	7.6
6	40	2	6.67
7	41	1	5.86

mixer, utensils, and oven. In the short run, the baker uses these pieces of equipment but does not alter their quantity. This assumption means that the baker does not vary the level of physical capital as production increases.

To increase the production of bread in the short run, the baker employs more workers. When L increases, Q increases. But the relationship between the two variables depends on the production process (Table 6.1).

Total product is the maximum amount of output that results from the employment of economic resources. In the example, the total product is the number of loaves of bread that the baker brings to the market. The Table 6.1 shows that, as labor increases, the total product increases. With the baker as the sole laborer, the business produces 10 units of output (loaves of bread) in a given period of time. But with two workers, the business produces 22 units of output. As the business employs more workers, output rises.

The *marginal product of labor* is the change in total product (ΔQ) divided by the change in labor input (ΔL). With the first worker, the total product increases from zero loaves of bread to 10 loaves of bread. The *MPL* for the first worker is therefore $\Delta Q \div \Delta L = 10 \div 1 = 10$. When the firm employs the second worker, the total product increases from 10 units of output to 22 units of output. The *MPL* of the second worker is therefore $\Delta Q \div \Delta L = 12 \div 1 = 12$. In this example, the change in labor in the denominator equals one.

When the firm employs a second worker, *increasing marginal returns* occur. The second worker contributes more to the production of output than the first worker. However, after the second worker, *diminishing marginal returns* sets in. As the firm employs more labor inputs, each worker contributes less to the production of output.

This pattern typically occurs in the short run when one economic resource is fixed. As the firm adds more labor to a fixed amount of physical capital, less workspace and a crowded production process lead to a reduction in the marginal productivity of labor. In the table, as more labor is added, marginal productivity declines. Note that it is possible for the marginal product of labor to reach zero and become negative. Firms, however, do not hire labor to this point.

The *average product of labor* is the total product divided by the quantity of labor input. This calculation serves as a measure of productivity. With the first worker, the business produces 10 units of output, so the $APL = Q \div L = 10 \div 1 = 10$. With the second worker, the business produces 22 units of output, so $APL = 22 \div 2 = 11$. With additional workers, the table demonstrates an increase in the APL and then a decrease. This pattern normally occurs.

PRODUCTION IN THE LONG RUN

In the long run, firms may adjust their economic resources. All economic resources are variable. In the example, the firm may alter its productive capacity, adjust its level of physical capital, and adapt according to market conditions. With the production function, rather than having a fixed level of capital ($\bar{K}$), production in the long run is a function of the variable economic resource inputs: $Q = f(L, K)$. In the long run, the firm adopts the technology that leads to the production of output at the lowest cost. With a different quantity of both labor and capital, the firm establishes a new method in which to turn economic resources inputs into output. In the bread-baking example, the new production process may entail a bigger oven, new utensils, and a larger mixer. These adjustments allow the baker to adapt to changing market conditions, including an increase in the demand for freshly baked bread.

COST

The first cost concept that characterizes the production process is *TC*. The *TC* is the cost of all economic resources used in production. Total cost equals total fixed cost (*TFC*) plus total variable cost

(TVC): $TC = TFC + TVC$. The TFC is the cost of fixed economic resources. In the short run, when the firm pays a fixed cost, such as a monthly rent payment, the cost does not change as output changes. The TVC is the cost of variable economic resources, such as labor. If the firm employs more workers when production increases, the TVC increases.

SHORT-RUN COST

As shown in Table 6.2, the cost of physical capital, the fixed economic resource in the short run, is $20 per hour. The wage paid to labor, the variable economic resource in the short run, is $15 per hour. Because the TVC increases with the quantity of labor, the TC also rises.

The second cost concept that characterizes the production process is MC. MC is the change in TC that results from the production of one more unit of output: $MC = \dfrac{\Delta TC}{\Delta Q}$. This information informs the firm about the cost of an additional unit of production. In the table, when the firm employs the first laborer, output increases from zero to 10 units. This information is in the total product column. But when output increases to 10 units, TC increases from $20 to $35,

Table 6.2 Cost for the firm

Labor	Total product (Q)	Total variable cost ($)	Total fixed cost ($)	Total cost ($)	Marginal cost ($)	Average total cost ($)
0	0	0	20	20	–	–
1	10	15	20	35	1.5	3.5
2	22	30	20	50	1.25	2.27
3	30	45	20	65	1.88	2.17
4	35	60	20	80	3	2.29
5	38	75	20	95	5	2.38
6	40	90	20	110	7.5	2.68
7	41	105	20	125	15	3.05

a difference of \$15. Therefore, the MC is: $MC = \dfrac{\Delta TC}{\Delta Q} = \dfrac{15}{10} = 1.5$. When the firm employs the second laborer, the total product increases from 10 to 22 units of output. At the same time, TC increases from \$35 to \$50. Therefore, $MC = \dfrac{\Delta TC}{\Delta Q} = \dfrac{15}{12} = 1.25$. The other calculations are in the MC column.

The third cost concept that characterizes the production process is *average cost*, which includes *average fixed cost* (AFC), *average variable cost* (AVC), and *average total cost* (ATC). Starting with $TC = TFC + TVC$, the calculation for average cost occurs by dividing by output:

$$\frac{TC}{Q} = \frac{TFC}{Q} + \frac{TVC}{Q}$$

or $ATC = AFC + AVC$. The last column in the table demonstrates how ATC changes as output rises.

Figure 6.1 demonstrates the normal shapes of the MC and average cost curves. The MC curve intersects the ATC and AVC at the minimum points of ATC and AVC. When MC is less than the average cost, the average cost is decreasing. When MC is greater than the average cost, the average cost is increasing.

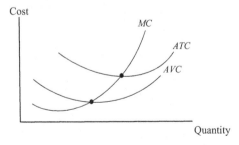

Figure 6.1 Marginal cost and average cost

LONG-RUN COST

In the long run, the firm varies its economic resources. The change in long-run cost is a function of the firm's production function, which determines the relationship between economic resources and output. In the bread-baking example, the firm determines that alternative forms of production create different average costs. In addition, different production capabilities create the ability to bring more bread to the market.

In the long run, the firm determines the level of production at the lowest ATC. The long-run ATC curve (ATC_{LR}) demonstrates the relationship between the production of output and the lowest attainable ATC (Figure 6.2). The long-run average cost curve serves as a planning curve, establishing the production process and quantity of economic resources to both produce output and minimize cost. Once the firm chooses the production process, such as the space the baker needs to produce output, the firm uses the cost curve that applies to the range of production.

ECONOMIES AND DISECONOMIES OF SCALE

Over specific ranges of production, the firm's technology leads to a change in ATC (Figure 6.2). If ATC decreases when output increases, the firm experiences *economies of scale*. In this range, the firm reaps cost advantages when it becomes more efficient. The two main reasons that economies of scale occur are *specialization* and

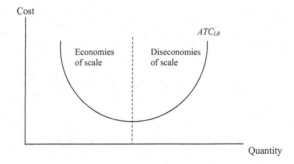

Figure 6.2 Long-run average total cost curve

the *division of labor*. The former occurs when workers focus their skills and talent on specific areas of production. The latter occurs when firms organize the economic tasks so that the workers specialize. While the baker bakes, the firm hires additional workers to take orders and deliver bread. This production process takes advantage of both specialization and division of labor. If *ATC* increases when output rises, however, the firm experiences *diseconomies of scale*. With organizational diseconomies of scale, the firm struggles to manage a growing workforce. With technical diseconomies of scale, the firm experiences internal constraints. With external diseconomies of scale, the market imposes constraints on production.

PROFIT

The firm's goal is to maximize economic profit, which equals *TR* minus *TC*. The *TR* equals the price of output multiplied by the quantity of output sold. The *TC* equals the opportunity cost of production.

TOTAL PROFIT AND THE SUPPLY DECISION

Suppose a loaf of bread sells for $7. With this price, the *TR* is calculated as follows: $TR = P \times Q$. Table 6.3 returns to the short run with the quantity of labor, total product, *TR*, *TC*, and profit, assuming labor is a variable economic resource and physical capital is a fixed economic resource. When the firm employs up to five workers, profit increases. With additional workers, production increases by a small amount, but profit decreases. Therefore, profit maximization occurs at five workers and 38 loaves of bread.

MARGINAL ANALYSIS AND THE SUPPLY DECISION

Marginal analysis establishes a way to find the profit-maximizing level of output, comparing the *MR* of an additional unit of output with the *MC* (Figure 6.3). If the $MR > MC$ as output rises, the profit increases. If the $MC > MR$ as output rises, the profit decreases. Therefore, the firm increases output to the point where $MR = MC$, the point of profit maximization. If the price of bread is

Table 6.3 Total revenue, total cost, and profit

Labor	Total product (Q)	Total revenue ($)	Total cost ($)	Profit (TR−TC)
0	0	0	20	−20
1	10	70	35	35
2	22	154	50	104
3	30	210	65	145
4	35	245	80	165
5	38	266	95	171
6	40	280	110	170
7	41	287	125	162

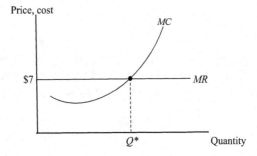

Figure 6.3 Profit maximization

$7, MR is constant when output increases. The profit-maximizing level of output occurs at Q*.

It is also possible to identify the profit-maximizing level of output by comparing the numerical values of MR and MC. The rules are as follows:

- If MR > MC, increase output.
- If MR < MC, decrease output.

Table 6.4 includes MR, MC, and profit. As the firm employs up to five workers, MR > MC. With four workers, total product = 35 units of output, MR = $7, and MC = $3. Because MR > MC, the firm hires another worker. With six workers, total product = 40 units of output, MR = $7, and MC = $7.5. Because MR < MC, the firm hires fewer workers. With five workers and 38 units of output, the firm maximizes profit. In this example, profit maximization

Table 6.4 Marginal revenue, marginal cost, and profit maximization

Labor	Total product (Q)	Total revenue ($)	Marginal revenue ($)	Total cost ($)	Marginal cost ($)	Profit (TR–TC)
0	0	0	–	20	–	−20
1	10	70	7	35	1.5	35
2	22	154	7	50	1.25	104
3	30	210	7	65	1.88	145
4	35	245	7	80	3	165
5	38	266	7	95	5	171
6	40	280	7	110	7.5	170
7	41	287	7	125	15	162

occurs at the level of output where *MR* is closest to *MC* without *MR* exceeding *MC*.

KEY TERMS

allocative efficiency
average cost
average fixed cost
average product of labor
average total cost
average variable cost
corporation
diminishing marginal returns
division of labor
economies of scale
firms
increasing marginal returns
long run
marginal cost
marginal product of labor
partnership
production function
productive efficiency
short run
sole proprietorship
specialization

technology
total cost
total product

FURTHER READING

Bandiera, Oriana, Elsayed, Ahmed, Smurra, Andrea and Zipfel, Celine. 2022. "Young Adults and Labor Markets in Africa." *Journal of Economic Perspectives*, 36(1): 81–100.

Barrero, Jose, Bloom, Nicholas and Davis, Steven. 2023. "The Evolution of Work from Home." *Journal of Economic Perspectives*, 37(4): 23–50.

Hortacsu, Ali and Syverson, Chad. 2015. "The Ongoing Evolution of US Retail: A Format of Tug-of-War." *Journal of Economic Perspectives*, 29(4): 89–112.

7

PERFECT COMPETITION

MARKET CLASSIFICATION

In markets, buyers and sellers interact in different ways. On the demand side, when consumers purchase goods and services online, they evaluate their options, seek information on quality and price, and attempt to make informed decisions. But, with face-to-face transactions, consumers speak with sales associates to inform their choices.

On the supply side, some industries are associated with *advertising*, the act of calling attention to goods or services in the market. Examples include entertainment, fashion, food, retail, and vehicles. Successful forms of advertising increase market demand by informing, persuading, and reminding customers to purchase specific forms of output. Evolving to take advantage of social media, technology, and market influencers, advertising creates awareness of brands, products, and services. A successful influencer on social media increases the demand for a specific good or service. But additional expenditure on advertising raises the ATC of the firm. When formulating an advertising budget, the firm weighs the benefit of greater consumer awareness against the cost.

The firms in some industries have been able to sustain economic profits. In the technology sector, Microsoft, Google, and Apple serve as examples. In social media, Meta maintains a profit through research and development. In software design, Nvidia, a multinational corporation, earns a profit from the production of programming interfaces, graphics processing units, and chips for mobile computing.

DOI: 10.4324/9781003533115-9

But the firms in industries that sell homogeneous products often struggle to break even. An example is an industrial farm that relies on government subsidies to cover the cost of production. Another example is a t-shirt shop in a tourist district that offers the same products as its rivals. A final example is a food truck in a line of food trucks that provides the same items, charging the same price as its competitors. In these examples, advertising may not serve as an important part of the business. A successful period of time is one in which sales cover the cost of production, including the wage for the business owner, thus establishing a break-even position.

Market structure refers to an industry classification that is determined by three characteristics: the number of sellers in the market, whether the product is standardized or differentiated, and if there are barriers that prevent the firms from entering or leaving the industry. These characteristics allow economists to classify industries into different categories.

This system of classification is important because it provides insights into both the functioning of the industry and the theory of the firm. Large firms such as Microsoft, Google, and Apple experience different market conditions than small firms working in clothing, hair styling, or the restaurant industry. The market conditions encourage the firms to make specific decisions with respect to pricing, production, and quality management. This chapter provides the first example in the book of market structure: perfect competition. Specifically, the chapter analyzes the characteristics of perfect competition, production decisions of the firm, perfectly competitive firms in the short run, and perfectly competitive firms in the long run.

CHARACTERISTICS OF PERFECT COMPETITION

Perfectly competitive markets offer a useful starting point for the analysis of market structure. The reason is the typical firm experiences so much competition that it does not have any influence over market price. As a result, the typical firm in perfect competition is a *price taker*, charging a price that is established in the market. A perfectly competitive market satisfies three conditions:

- A large number of sellers exist. Each sells a small fraction of the output in the market

- Sellers offer a standardized product
- There are no significant barriers that restrict sellers from entering or exiting the market

LARGE NUMBER OF SELLERS

In perfectly competitive markets, the number of sellers is so large that no business alters the price by changing the amount that is sold. For example, with industrial agriculture, there are thousands of farmers who grow corn. While the farms consist of hundreds or thousands of acres, each farmer grows a small percentage of the total output in the market. Even if a farmer doubles its level of production, there is no impact on market price.

STANDARDIZED PRODUCT

Perfectly competitive markets provide a homogeneous product. Consumers do not perceive a difference between the products that they buy. With industrial agriculture, the buyers that purchase corn in order to make corn syrup do not perceive a difference between the standardized product. They are willing to purchase the product from any seller. The same holds true for wheat and soybeans. In markets for other commodities, including gold, silver, stocks, and bonds, the sellers offer a standardized product. A share of stock sold by a stockbroker is indistinguishable from a share of stock of the same company sold by a different stockbroker. If the consumers perceive a difference in the form of output, the market is not perfectly competitive.

NO SIGNIFICANT MARKET BARRIERS

Markets experience changing economic conditions. In the absence of significant market barriers, firms may enter the market during periods of economic profit and exit during periods of loss. During the coronavirus pandemic, for example, in 2020, many firms closed and exited their industries because of the downturn in economic activity. But to enter a market when economic conditions are favorable, firms incur costs by purchasing economic resources, establishing production processes, and making contacts with customers. Despite the presence of these costs, perfectly competitive markets do not establish significant barriers to entry. The assumption is that any firm that wants to enter a perfectly competitive market experiences the same economic conditions as firms that are already in the market. A farmer who wants to start farming corn experiences the same costs for land, labor, and farm equipment as existing farms. But markets that are not perfectly competitive possess barriers to entry, including capital requirements, economies of scale, legal barriers, product differentiation, and zoning laws. When significant barriers exist, the market is not perfectly competitive.

PRODUCTION DECISIONS OF THE FIRM

A market consists of a collection of buyers and sellers. The interaction between supply and demand establishes an equilibrium price and quantity. Because supply and demand change, the buyers and sellers react to different market conditions. An increase in the supply of firms, for example, decreases market price, lowers the economic profit of the typical firm, and makes the product more affordable for consumers. An increase in market demand, in contrast, increases the market price, raises the economic profit of the typical firm, and makes the product less affordable for consumers.

Figure 7.1 provides two graphs: one for a t-shirt market in perfect competition with upward-sloping supply (S) and downward-sloping demand (D) and another for the typical firm, a t-shirt shop.

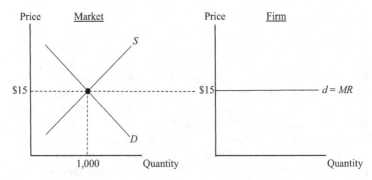

Figure 7.1 The perfectly competitive market and firm

The market establishes an equilibrium price of $15 per t-shirt and an equilibrium quantity of 1,000 t-shirts. Because the typical firm in perfect competition is a price taker, the firm charges $15 per t-shirt. If the market establishes a different per unit price, the firm would take this new price as a given. The price-taking characteristic establishes a perfectly elastic (horizontal) demand curve for the firm (d). The perfectly competitive firm sells all the output it wants at the market price, but it cannot sell any output at a higher price.

In the t-shirt market, the output is standardized. If one t-shirt shop charges $20 and all the other shops charge $15, no one will buy t-shirts for the higher price. As the following analysis reveals, when the price is constant and demand is perfectly elastic, price equals MR. For the firm, the question becomes how many t-shirts to sell, which depends on revenue and cost.

REVENUE AND COST

Table 7.1 shows the revenue and cost data for the t-shirt shop. When output increases, the price remains constant, reflecting the perfectly elastic demand curve. Total revenue (TR) is calculated by multiplying the per unit price by the quantity of output. MR is calculated by dividing the change in TR by the change in output. For each unit of output, TC is given. But MC equals the change in TC divided by the change in output. Profit is TR minus TC. With this data, the firm identifies the profit-maximizing level of output.

PROFIT-MAXIMIZING LEVEL OF OUTPUT

The objective of the firm is to maximize profit. To satisfy the objective, the firm identifies the profit-maximizing level of output (q^*). As Chapter 6 explains, there are two ways to find q^*, the TR/TC approach and the MR/MC approach. Table 7.1 provides the data for both approaches. The first approach is to calculate profit at each level of output. Because profit = $TR - TC$, profit is maximized at eight units of output. The second approach is for the firm to increase output as long as MR is greater than MC. When MR equals MC, profit is maximized. After this point, profit declines when the firm produces more output. This approach also yields the profit-maximizing level of output of eight units (Figure 7.2).

Table 7.1 Revenue, cost, and profit data for the perfectly-competitive firm

Total product (output)	Price ($)	Total revenue ($)	Marginal revenue ($)	Total cost ($)	Marginal cost ($)	Profit ($)
0	15	0	–	25	–	−25
1	15	15	15	45	20	−30
2	15	30	15	55	10	−25
3	15	45	15	63	8	−18
4	15	60	15	69	6	−9
5	15	75	15	73	4	2
6	15	90	15	75	2	15
7	15	105	15	87	12	18
8	15	120	15	100	13	20
9	15	135	15	120	20	15
10	15	150	15	145	25	5

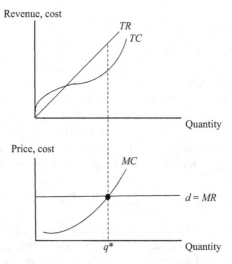

Figure 7.2 Profit-maximizing level of output for the firm

PROFIT PER UNIT

At q^*, it is possible to calculate the level of profit per unit, which equals price (P) minus ATC:

$$\text{Profit per unit} = P - ATC.$$

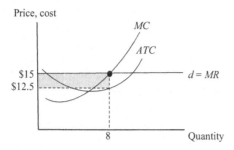

Figure 7.3 Profit per unit

When $q^* = 8$, the profit maximizing level of output, the price equals \$15 per unit. The ATC is calculated by dividing TC by output: $ATC = TC/Q = \$100/8 = \$12.5$. The profit per unit equals \$15 − \$12.5 = \$2.5. In Figure 7.3, the profit per unit equals the vertical distance between d and the ATC at eight units of output.

Total profit equals profit per unit times the number of units sold:

$$\text{Total profit} = (P - ATC)(q^*).$$

In the example, total profit = (\$15 − \$12.5)(8) = (\$2.5)(8) = \$20, which is the same calculation in Table 7.1. In Figure 7.3, the shaded rectangle represents the profit. As long as the price is greater than ATC at the profit maximizing level of output, the firm is earning a profit. If, however, the price is less than ATC at q^*, the firm is experiencing a loss. When the price equals ATC at q^*, the firm is breaking even.

- When $P > ATC$ at q^*, the firm earns a profit
- When $P < ATC$ at q^*, the firm experiences a loss
- When $P = ATC$ at q^*, the firm breaks even

In each case, q^* is the optimal level of production.

THE FIRM'S SHORT-RUN SUPPLY CURVE

In perfect competition, the firm acts as a price taker, charging the price that is established in the market. If the market price changes, the firm's price changes. In this case, the firm identifies a new profit-maximizing level of output. As shown in Figure 7.4, three demand curves correspond to three market prices. At each price, the firm equates MR with MC to find the profit-maximizing level of output. With a change in price, the firm operates along the MC curve to identify how much output to produce. When the price is P_1, for example, the firm produces q_1^* units of output. When the price decreases, the firm produces less. The firm's supply curve is the shaded line.

If the firm is suffering a loss, however, it will not operate along the MC curve. It will produce zero units of output. This is the *shutdown rule*. If $MR = MC$ and TR is less than TVC, the firm is not covering its operating costs. In this case, the firm should shut down. On a per-unit basis, the firm's shutdown condition is the following:

$$\text{Shut down when } TR/q < TVC/q.$$

Another way to formulate the shutdown rule is to note that the left-hand side is revenue per unit, which is equal to price (P). The right-hand side is the firm's AVC. The firm should shut down in the following situation:

$$\text{Shut down when } P < AVC.$$

As shown in Figure 7.4, the shutdown decision occurs at P_3. At this price, the firm must decide whether or not to stay in business.

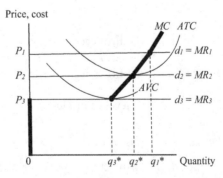

Figure 7.4 The firm's supply curve and shutdown rule

Note that the shutdown price occurs at the minimum point of the AVC curve, where $MC = AVC$. If the price falls below P_3, the firm should shut down. Between the prices of P_2 and P_3, however, the firm suffers a loss but covers its operating costs. In this range, the firm hopes to stay in business until market conditions improve. In summary, a perfectly competitive firm's supply curve is equal to the MC curve above the minimum point of AVC. Below this point, the firm produces zero units of output.

PERFECTLY COMPETITIVE FIRMS IN THE SHORT RUN

The short run is a period of time in which the typical firm does not have the opportunity to vary its fixed economic resources. In the short run, an insufficient amount of time exists for a new firm to acquire fixed economic resources and enter the market even if the typical firm is earning a profit. At the same time, an insufficient amount of time exists for firms to decrease their fixed economic resources to zero and exit the market with a loss. Therefore, in the short run, the number of firms in the industry is fixed. In addition, the typical firm earns a profit or experiences a loss.

The market demand and supply curves appear in Figure 7.1. The intersection of the market demand and market supply curves determines the price for the typical firm.

On the demand side, the market demand curve is the summation of the consumption choices of individual consumers at each market price. At a specific price, the consumers in the market will be willing and able to purchase a certain number of t-shirts.

On the supply side, the supply curve of the individual firm is the same as the MC curve above the minimum of AVC. The short-run market supply curve is determined by summing the quantities of all firms in the industry at each price. At a specific price, the firms in the industry are willing and able to sell a certain number of t-shirts. Along the market supply curve, both the number of firms and fixed economic resources are constant.

PERFECTLY COMPETITIVE FIRMS IN THE LONG RUN

The long-run time horizon is sufficient for firms to vary all of their economic resources. This list includes the machines, equipment, and plants. A firm may reconfigure its production process, become more capital intensive, or enlarge its productive capacity. It may also reduce its physical presence by selling online. In the long run, firms have the opportunity to adjust their production processes according to market conditions. But the long run is also a time frame in which new firms may acquire economic resources and enter the market. If the typical firm is earning a profit, this option occurs. At the same time, the long run provides a time frame in which existing firms may sell their economic resources and exit the market. Recall that an important assumption in perfect competition is the lack of economic barriers for entry or exit. What is the impetus for entering or exiting the industry? The presence of economic profit for the typical firm signals new firms to enter the industry. But an economic loss for the typical firm serves as the driving force for an exit.

LONG-RUN EQUILIBRIUM

As this chapter explains, economic profit is equal to the amount that TR exceeds all of the costs of production. The latter includes the costs of economic resource inputs and the foregone income or investment income for an entrepreneur who allocates money and time to the firm. As a result, when firms experience an economic profit, the entrepreneurs earn more than they would by allocating their time and money to alternative economic activities.

A period of economic profit for the typical firm does not alter a perfectly competitive market, besides the satisfaction flowing to the entrepreneur. But if an economic profit for the typical firm reflects fundamental market conditions, the industry will change. If a t-shirt shop earns an economic profit because it is supplying a product in demand, entrepreneurs will join the industry. Because there are no barriers to entry, this option exists.

In contrast, if existing firms experience economic losses, their TR is insufficient to cover all of the costs of production. Other industries may provide better opportunities for their money and time. If an economic loss is forecasted for the typical firm over the long-run planning horizon when it may vary its economic resources, the firm will exit the industry. It will sell its machines, equipment, and plant, thus reducing its economic loss to zero.

In perfect competition, the presence of economic profit or loss serves as the driving force for change in the long run. If the forecast is for a future economic profit, more firms will enter the industry. In addition, existing firms may add new product lines. If the forecast is for a future economic loss, firms will exit the industry. The firms may choose to eliminate an unprofitable product line. In perfectly competitive markets, these conditions create the long-run equilibrium.

In Figure 7.5, the short-run market supply curve (S_1) establishes an economic profit for the typical firm at a price of $15. If no firms enter the market, the profit remains. In the long run, however, the market conditions change. The profit of the typical firm attracts new businesses. When new firms enter the market, the market supply curve shifts rightward to S_2. The quantity of output in the market increases from 1,000 to 1,200 t-shirts. The market price decreases to $10. When the market price decreases, the horizontal demand curve of the firm shifts down from d_1 to d_2. The firm moves down its MC curve, reducing its output from eight to six units. The process continues until the typical firm is no longer earning an economic profit. This long-run equilibrium occurs at the minimum point of ATC. The equilibrium position means the ATC curve becomes the long-run average total cost curve $(LRATC)$.

ZERO ECONOMIC PROFIT IN THE LONG RUN

Even though the typical firm in perfect competition breaks even in the long run, the market structure has its merits. The break-even position is the same as zero economic profit: TR equals all of the

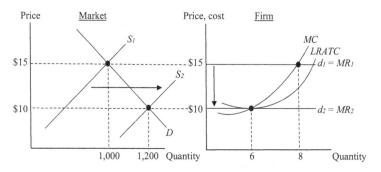

Figure 7.5 Firms enter the industry

costs of production. But zero economic profit includes the compensation flowing to the entrepreneur for any foregone investment income. As a result, economists use the term *normal profit* to mean zero economic profit or break even, emphasizing that the long-run equilibrium position in perfect competition exists as a viable outcome.

EFFICIENCY CONDITIONS FOR PERFECT COMPETITION

In economics, the concept of efficiency means that firms allocate resources to their most productive uses. A method of evaluating market structures is to consider whether firms achieve two types of efficiency: allocative efficiency and productive efficiency. The perfectly competitive firm achieves both forms of efficiency. Allocative efficiency occurs when the firm is producing the output that consumers want. This efficiency condition exists if the firm is producing at the point where price equals MC. In perfect competition, this condition holds because of the horizontal demand curve of the firm. Equating MR with MC means that $P = MC$. Productive efficiency occurs when the firm produces output at the lowest cost. This efficiency condition exists if the firm is producing at the point where price equals the minimum point of ATC. In perfect competition, the long-run equilibrium position guarantees that the firm moves to the point where $P = \min ATC$. In the other market structures, the efficiency conditions do not hold.

A CHANGE IN MARKET CONDITIONS

This chapter on perfect competition discusses competitive markets, market characteristics, how firms make production decisions, and different time frames. What happens when market conditions change?

A CHANGE IN MARKET DEMAND

The market demand curve may increase or decrease (shift right or left), according to changes in consumer behavior. If the market is operating at the long-run equilibrium, the firm starts at the break-even position of zero economic profit. Suppose the consumers

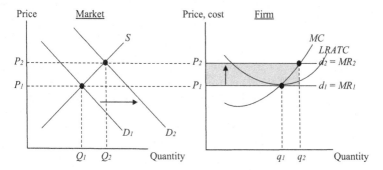

Figure 7.6 Increase in market demand

increase their tastes and preferences for t-shirts. In Figure 7.6, the market demand curve shifts to the right from D_1 to D_2, increasing market price from P_1 to P_2 and market quantity from Q_1 to Q_2. The perfectly elastic demand curve of the firm shifts from d_1 to d_2. For the firm, three important outcomes occur: the per unit price increases from P_1 to P_2; the quantity of output increases from q_1 to q_2; and economic profit increases from zero to a positive amount (shaded area). Because economic profit exists, however, more firms will enter the industry in the long run, the supply curve will shift right, and the economy will return to the long-run equilibrium (break-even) position at a price of P_1.

A CHANGE IN MARKET SUPPLY

The market supply curve may increase or decrease (shift right or left), according to changes in economic conditions. In industries such as agriculture, food provision, and retail, technological change impacts how firms turn economic resources into output. In t-shirt markets, suppliers may print t-shirts on demand, deliver t-shirts in more cost-effective ways, and interact with consumers using multiple platforms. In Figure 7.7, a technological advance means the long-run average cost curve decreases from $LRATC_1$ to $LRATC_2$. In the absence of the MC curve on the graph, the firm chooses a profit-maximizing level of output (q^*). In the long run, economic profit leads to two outcomes. First, the firms in the industry have the incentive to adopt the new technology. In a perfectly

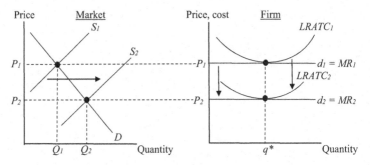

Figure 7.7 Increase in market supply

competitive market, no barriers prevent firms from adopting tech-nological advances. As all suppliers in the market adopt the new forms of technology, $LRATC_1$ decreases to $LRATC_2$. Second, new firms have the incentive to enter the market, while adopting tech-nological advances. The result is an increase in the market supply curve from S_1 to S_2, a decrease in price from P_1 to P_2, and a move-ment to the long-run position of zero economic profit when P_2 = minimum $LRATC_2$.

Any firm that does not adopt the new technology will expe-rience an economic loss and exit the industry. Because the firms in the industry adopt technological advances, the profits return to zero. While the production costs decrease, the consumers benefit from a lower price.

MARKET SIGNALS AND ECONOMIC ACTIVITY

The changes in market demand and market supply create new eco-nomic outcomes. If the market demand curve increases, it shifts to the right, initially increasing the price. This change leads to eco-nomic profit for the typical firm. But the economic profit encour-ages new firms to enter the industry. The market supply curve increases and shifts to the right until price returns to its original position. The long-run equilibrium is a return to the break-even point.

If the market demand curve decreases, it shifts to the left, initially decreasing price. This change leads to a loss for the typical firm.

The loss encourages firms to exit the industry. The market supply curve decreases and shifts to the left until price returns to its original point. The long-run equilibrium is a return to the break-even position.

If the market supply curve increases from a technological advance, the *LRATC* curve of the typical firm decreases. When the market price is greater than *ATC* at the optimal level of production, the firm experiences an economic profit. But firms enter the industry, shifting the market supply curve to the right until price is equal to the minimum point of *ATC*, a return to break even.

If the market supply curve decreases, the *LRATC* curve of the typical firm increases. When the market price is less than *ATC* at the optimal level of production, the firm experiences a loss. But firms exit the industry, shifting the market supply curve to the left until price is equal to the minimum point of *ATC*, a return to break even.

KEY TERMS

advertising
market structure
normal profit
price taker
shutdown rule

FURTHER READING

Makowski, Louis and Ostroy, Joseph. 2001. "Perfect Competition and the Creativity of the Market." *Journal of Economic Perspectives*, 39(2): 479–535.
McDermott, John. 2015. "Perfect Competition, Methodologically Contemplated." *Journal of Post Keynesian Economics*, 37(4), 687–703.

8

MONOPOLY

A SPECTRUM OF COMPETITION

Chapter 7 on perfect competition explains that the typical firm in the industry has no market power. With its production decisions, it cannot alter market price. Because the perfectly competitive firm provides a homogeneous product, it does not advertise. Perfect competition exists on one end of the competitive spectrum. On the other end of the spectrum is a *monopoly*, when one firm constitutes the entire industry. In the United States, antitrust laws prohibit firms from exhibiting monopoly power if they restrict market competition. The motivation for this legal reality is that monopolies have the power to raise the price and restrict quantity.

But *natural monopolies* may exist, although they are regulated by the government. A natural monopoly exists as a barrier to entry into a specific industry. In this case, a single firm serves the entire market. With a natural monopoly, the average cost curves exhibit economies of scale at all levels of output. Graphically, the natural monopolist's *ATC* curve is always declining. As the firm produces more output, its *ATC* decreases, even in the case when the firm produces all of the output in the industry. Dividing output among several firms would increase the *ATC* of production.

The common examples of natural monopolies are utilities and waste management. A local utility supplies electricity to buildings in the power grid. A firm working in waste management collects the garbage in a community and takes it to a garbage dump. In these cases, the natural monopolist provides the service at a lower average cost than the competitors. That is, the firm's average costs decrease

DOI: 10.4324/9781003533115-10

when the firm produces more output. This outcome results from the high physical capital investment necessary to operate in the industry.

Search engines offer another example. By the beginning of this century, Google established a popular search engine. By the third decade of this century, Google handled over 90 percent of the search queries worldwide. The services provided by Google's parent company Alphabet include Chrome, Gmail, Google Docs, and YouTube. These services keep consumers engaged in communication, entertainment, the search for information, and work. But consumers may use the services for free. To generate revenue, the company sells advertising for firms that have their websites appear on Web searches. With over a billion users worldwide, Alphabet generates a significant amount of advertising revenue on a daily basis.

Market structure establishes three characteristics: the number of sellers, whether the product is standardized or differentiated, and if barriers prevent firms from entering or exiting the industry. In the monopoly market, one seller exists. The product is standardized with no close substitutes. For example, electricity is the same regardless of the source. The possibility of installing solar panels exists as a costly alternative. In a monopoly market, advertising may or may not occur. With utilities, customers receive information about the rate, seasonal changes in demand, and other market conditions. Because no competition exists, the natural monopolist does not advertise to differentiate its product. Significant barriers exist. To discuss the characteristics of the monopoly market, this chapter addresses the sources of market power, production decisions of a monopoly, comparison between monopoly and competition, price discrimination, and regulation and antitrust policy.

SOURCES OF MARKET POWER

When firms have market power, they have some control over price. When moving from perfect competition to monopoly, market power increases. In an industry, a monopoly exhibits the maximum amount of market power, which stems from the barriers to entry. The barriers to entry take three forms. First, a firm may have a significant amount of control over a factor of production, such as a professional sports league that has exclusive rights to draft players. Second, the economies of scale provide a competitive advantage.

With this advantage, market power occurs when firms are discouraged from entering the industry. Third, the government may establish barriers to entry through *copyrights*, *franchises*, and *patents*. A copyright is an exclusive right to film, perform, print, publish, or record an artistic, literary, or musical piece. A franchise is a government authorization for an economic activity, such as serving as an agent or broadcasting a program. A patent exists when the government grants a property right to an inventor of a new idea, process, or product. When barriers to entry exist in a monopoly market, firms cannot enter.

PRODUCTION DECISIONS OF A MONOPOLY

Chapters 6 and 7 established that the optimal level of production for the firm occurs where MR equals MC. When the price is greater than ATC, a profit exists. When the price is less than ATC, a loss exists. Although the monopolist may adjust output, it produces at the optimal level where $MR = MC$. But in producing at this point, the monopoly faces a downward-sloping demand curve. This shape differs from the demand curve facing the firm in perfect competition, which is perfectly elastic (horizontal). The reason the monopolist faces a downward-sloping demand curve is that it must lower the price in order to sell additional units of output. This is the Law of Demand. But when the demand curve is downward-sloping, the MR is less than the price (Figure 8.1).

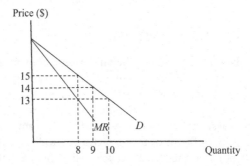

Figure 8.1 Demand, price, and marginal revenue for the monopolist

To demonstrate that $MR < P$, consider both the quantity demanded and TR. Price is determined along the demand curve. The Law of Demand says that when price decreases, quantity demanded increases:

- At a price of $15, quantity demanded equals eight units of output, so $TR = (P)(Q) = (\$15)(8) = \$120$.
- At a price of $14, quantity demanded equals nine units of output, so $TR = (P)(Q) = (\$14)(9) = \$126$.
- At a price of $13, quantity demanded equals ten units of output, so $TR = (P)(Q) = (\$13)(10) = \$130$.

When quantity increases by one unit, MR equals the change in TR divided by the change in output. When the quantity of output increases from eight to nine units, $MR = \Delta TR/\Delta Q = (\$126 - \$120)/(9 - 8) = \$6/1 = \$6$. When the quantity of output increases from nine to ten units, $MR = \Delta TR/\Delta Q = (\$130 - \$126)/(10 - 9) = \$4/1 = \$4$. As quantity increases, MR decreases. When demand slopes downward, MR is less than price. Mathematically, the MR curve falls twice as fast as the demand curve.

PROFIT MAXIMIZATION

The price that the monopolist charges depends on the level of output. This reality differs from the choice of the firm in perfect competition that takes the market price as a given. To find the optimal level of production (q^*), the monopolist produces where $MR = MC$. In Figure 8.2, $MR = MC$ at point a. At q^*, the monopolist sets the price (P_1) on the demand curve and finds the ATC_1 on the ATC curve. Because $P_1 > ATC_1$ at q^*, a profit exists (shaded area).

LOSS MINIMIZATION

The fact that a monopoly exists as the only firm in an industry does not guarantee that it will earn an economic profit. A monopolist experiences production costs, a downward-sloping demand curve, and a limit to the price in which it may charge. Therefore, to remain in business in the long run, a monopolist must at least break even (earn a normal profit). But in the short run, a loss means that the price is less than ATC (Figure 8.3). In this case, the monopolist

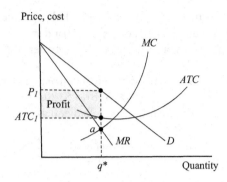

Figure 8.2 Profit maximization for the monopolist

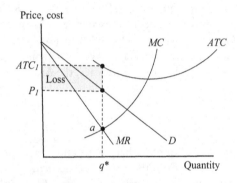

Figure 8.3 Loss minimization for the monopolist

produces where $MR = MC$ at point a; however, q^* becomes a point of loss minimization, not profit maximization. The shaded region is the loss rectangle.

COMPARISON BETWEEN MONOPOLY AND COMPETITION

There is one similarity and many differences between a perfectly competitive firm and a monopoly. The similarity is that they both choose to operate at the optimal level of production (q^*) where $MR = MC$. When price is greater than ATC, q^* is a profit-maximizing level of production. When price is less than *ATC*, q^* is a loss-minimizing level of production. When price is equal to *ATC*, q^* is a break-even level of production. But many differences exist. First, a perfectly competitive firm is a price taker, taking the price set in the market as a given. The monopolist is a price maker, establishing the industry price. Second, the perfectly competitive firm faces a perfectly elastic (horizontal) demand curve. The monopolist faces a downward-sloping demand curve. Third, given the same cost structure, a perfectly competitive firm will charge a lower price (P_C) and produce a higher quantity (q_C) when compared to a monopolist's price (P_M) and quantity (q_M).

In Figure 8.4, the *MC* curve is identical for the perfectly competitive firm and the monopoly (The *MC* curve is a straight line for the purpose of simplification). Because the demand curve facing the perfectly competitive firm on the left is horizontal, demand is equal to *MR*. The firm operates where *MR* = *MC*, leading to the competitive price and quantity of output. Because the demand curve facing the monopolist on the right is downward-sloping and demand ≠ *MR*, the pricing and output decisions are different. While the monopolist operates where *MR* = *MC*, the price is higher and the quantity of output is lower when compared to the firm in perfect competition.

The higher price and lower quantity for the monopolist lead to efficiency consequences. With the monopoly, consumers value

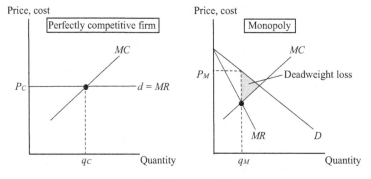

Figure 8.4 Price and quantity comparison between competition and monopoly

the quantity q_M at P_M, but the cost to produce this unit of output occurs where $MR = MC$. Because the consumer value is greater than the cost of this unit production, an efficiency loss exists with the monopoly. An additional economic benefit occurs at a higher level of output. In particular, the monopolist does not use MC pricing. But if it did, the monopolist's output would increase and price would decrease to the level of the perfectly competitive firm. The deadweight loss for the monopoly is the consumer surplus and producer surplus that is lost when the actual output is less than the efficient level of output (which occurs with perfect competition). With the monopoly, the deadweight loss is equal to the shaded area. In the market, the monopolist uses its market power to increase its producer surplus at the expense of the consumers, creating inefficiency in the form of deadweight loss.

RENT-SEEKING BEHAVIOR

When compared to competitive firms, monopolies charge higher prices and produce lower levels of output. These are the reasons that monopolies often maintain economic profit. Even though the behavior of monopolies generates a deadweight loss, they protect their profit. If the barriers to entry into the market ease, price declines, leading to a decrease in profit. This is the reason that, in perfect competition, there is always the possibility of new firms entering the market when profit exists. How do monopolies ensure that they do not experience market competition? Monopolies allocate resources to protect their monopoly status instead of allocating resources to produce higher levels of output. With this *rent seeking*, monopolies enhance their economic position without a contribution to productivity. This process occurs by hiring lobbyists to work with the government, seeking patents, or creating barriers to entry for other firms. But these activities are inefficient because they use economic resources in unproductive ways. From the perspective of the market, the rent-seeking behavior creates an efficiency loss. In addition to the rent-seeking behavior, society suffers from *x-inefficiency* when monopolies lack the incentive to control costs. Examples include hiring workers for political reasons, implementing employee perks, or scheduling corporate retreats. The outcome of x-inefficiency is an increase in the ATC.

INNOVATION

The existence of rent-seeking behavior and x-inefficiency demonstrates the costs to society from a high degree of market power. But through the provision of an important service, the development of a new product with the use of intellectual property, or the creation of a new technology, firms with market power may contribute to society. The idea is that the incentive to earn both monopoly status and economic profit encourages firms to invest in research and development. Otherwise, a firm would not have the incentive to allocate a large amount of its operating budget to a new good or service. The ability of a firm to enhance its level of market power through the process of innovation serves as an important economic force.

BENEFITS AND COSTS OF MONOPOLIES

For monopolies, do the benefits of innovation outweigh the costs of market power, including higher prices, lower output, rent-seeking behavior, and x-inefficiency? Most economists agree that the answer is no. Even though larger firms have more resources to allocate for research and development, contributing to the processes of innovation and technological advancement, the higher prices and lower levels of output lead to a deadweight loss. In monopoly markets, resources are allocated to maintain monopoly status, representing waste from an economic perspective.

PRICE DISCRIMINATION

With market power, firms may charge different prices to different customers for the same good or service. An example is charging students less money for a game or concert while charging adults more. This practice, *price discrimination*, increases the level of economic profit by converting some or all of the consumer surplus into producer surplus. If the market price of a game or concert is $50 but an individual is willing and able to pay $75, a ticket company may attempt to capture as much of the $25 surplus as possible. The reason that monopolies and other firms with market power undertake this process is that they have the ability to set the price. A perfectly competitive firm cannot price discriminate because it takes the market price as a given. For price discrimination to occur, three conditions must exist:

- The seller must have market power.
- The seller must have the ability to differentiate between consumers by sorting them into different groups according to their price elasticity of demand.
- The seller must prevent arbitrage when consumers purchase a product at a lower price and sell to other consumers at a higher price.

Different types of price discrimination exist. First-degree price discrimination occurs when firms charge each customer the maximum price that they are willing to pay. But sellers normally cannot charge a different price to each customer. Second-degree price discrimination occurs when firms charge different prices to consumers while focusing on quantity. An example is when a phone company charges a higher price when a consumer uses a certain number of minutes. Third-degree price discrimination occurs when firms charge different prices to different groups of consumers. This practice occurs when firms charge different prices to children, students, adults, and seniors for the same good or service.

The result of price discrimination is that some consumers pay a higher price than they would pay in a competitive market. Some consumers may even pay a higher price than what would exist in a monopoly market. But other consumers pay a lower price, such as seniors buying discounted tickets. With price discrimination, the firm captures additional market surplus.

REGULATION AND ANTITRUST POLICY

This chapter shows that monopolies charge higher prices and produce lower levels of output when compared to competitive firms. This reality places monopolies at the opposite end of the spectrum of competition from firms in perfectly competitive markets. Monopolies may also use their position in the market to price discriminate, earning additional producer surplus while decreasing consumer surplus. As a result of this anti-competitive behavior, the government implements both regulation and antitrust policy.

REGULATION

In special cases, a natural monopoly exists as a barrier to entry. When the economies of scale are sufficiently high, one firm should produce all of the output. In communities, public utilities and waste management serve as common examples. In a market, suppose a natural monopoly produces at a constant MC of \$15 per unit. Its fixed costs equal \$150. In this case, ATC decreases over the entire range of output. To demonstrate, recall that TC equals TFC plus TVC:

$$TC = TFC + TVC = 150 + 15Q.$$

To find the average cost, the TC is divided by the quantity of output (Q):

$$\frac{TC}{Q} = \frac{TFC}{Q} + \frac{TVC}{Q}$$

or $ATC = AFC + AVC$. In this example, $ATC = \dfrac{TC}{Q} = \dfrac{150 + 15Q}{Q} = \dfrac{150}{Q} + 15$. As the natural monopoly produces more output (Q), ATC decreases. If all of the firms in the industry have an identical cost structure, the least-cost method of production is for one firm to produce all of the output. More than one firm producing output would increase the average cost of the industry because each firm would experience fixed costs equal to \$150. The existence of one firm means that the fixed costs are not replicated across several firms. In industries such as waste management with high fixed costs and stable MC, the natural monopoly will grow, producing all of the industry's output.

Economists argue that electricity transmission serves as a natural monopoly. A high level of fixed cost exists for establishing a network of meters, substations, and transmission lines to support homes and businesses. After the network is established, however, the MC of producing an additional unit of electricity is low.

But the existence of complete market power with electricity transmission, waste management, and other natural monopolies incentivizes the government to regulate these firms through price/quantity restraints in the case of private ownership or government

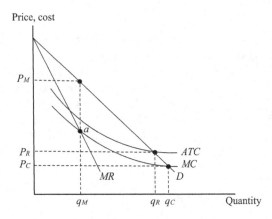

Figure 8.5 Regulation of a natural monopoly

control in the case of public ownership. Because of the economies of scale, the *ATC* and *MC* curves decline (Figure 8.5). If the
monopolist is a private firm with no regulation, it operates where
MR = *MC* at point *a*, earning an economic profit. The monopoly
price (P_M) is higher than the competitive price (P_C). The monopoly output (q_M) is less than the competitive output (q_C). Because of
the higher price and lower quantity, the government regulates the
natural monopoly. In this case, the government implements a *MC*
or *ATC* pricing rule.

With the *MC* pricing rule, regulators require the natural monopoly to operate where price = *MC* at P_C and q_C. This point leads to
an optimal level of resource allocation; however, it also generates
an economic loss at q_C because P_C < *ATC*. To keep the natural
monopoly in business, the government implements a subsidy equal
to the vertical distance between *ATC* and P_C. The subsidy creates
a socially optimal level of output for consumers while generating
a normal profit for the firm. Appealing from the perspective of
consumers, this option is costly from the perspective of the government. In the United States, the subsidies flowing to Amtrak that
generate competitive prices serve as an example of *MC* pricing in a
monopoly market.

With the *ATC* pricing rule, the regulation requires that the
monopolist produce q_R units of output and charge a price of P_R.

This rule, more common than MC pricing, puts the monopoly in a position to break even, earning a normal profit. Compared to the competitive position, the economic welfare for consumers is lower with the ATC pricing rule because they must pay a higher price and experience a lower level of output. But the break-even position with P_R keeps the monopolist in business, eliminating the need for a government subsidy.

ANTITRUST POLICY

Instead of regulating price and quantity, the government may implement a different approach: *antitrust policy*. This form of policy is designed to prevent monopoly power while preserving market competition. Many important antitrust cases have occurred for aluminum, oil, and railroads. In the United States, several statutes establish the country's antitrust laws, including the Sherman Act (1890), the Clayton Act (1914), and the Federal Trade Commission Act (1914). While stopping the spread of monopolies, antitrust policies prevent the inefficiencies that result from market power. The implication is that the antitrust policy exists as a method to promote competition. It also exists alongside other policies that favor government intervention through price and quantity controls. But the antitrust policy has not been as effective in promoting competitive markets because of long legal cases, the problem of establishing effective solutions for monopoly power, the difficulty in identifying when anti-competitive behavior reduces consumer welfare, and the challenge of implementing antitrust policy in markets with technological change.

EFFICIENCY CONDITIONS

When compared to a firm in perfect competition, a monopoly is less efficient. This chapter demonstrates that a monopoly charges a higher price and produces a lower level of output. In economics, a firm is operating efficiently if it is allocating economic resources in the most cost-effective and productive manner. Allocative efficiency means the firm is producing the output that consumers want. This form of efficiency exists when the firm is producing where price equals MC. In an unregulated monopoly market, this condition does not hold. In Figure 8.5, the market price of P_M is greater than MC at q_M. Productive efficiency occurs when the firm produces at the lowest ATC. In an unregulated monopoly market, this condition does not hold. At q_M in Figure 8.5, ATC is declining but not at a minimum. In sum, a monopoly generates less surplus than a firm in perfect competition, resulting in a deadweight loss.

KEY TERMS

antitrust policy
copyrights
franchises
monopoly
natural monopolies
patents
price discrimination
rent seeking
x-inefficiency

FURTHER READING

Gabel, David. 2016. "Uber and the Persistence of Market Power." *Journal of Economic Issues*, 50(2): 527–534.

Lamoreaux, Naomi. 2019. "The Problem of Bigness: From Standard Oil to Google." *Journal of Economic Perspectives*, 33(3): 94–117.

Shapiro, Carl. 2019. "Protecting Competition in the American Economy: Merger Control, Tech Titans, Labor Markets." *Journal of Economic Perspectives*, 33(3): 69–93.

9

OLIGOPOLY

MUTUAL INTERDEPENDENCE

In some industries, a small number of large firms produce most of the output. These firms are not monopolies, but they operate with a degree of market power that rivals the market power of monopolies. The firms are *oligopolies*. There are so few sellers that the decisions of one firm influence the decisions of others. For a long period of time, the three largest mobile network providers in the United States, AT&T, Verizon, and T-Mobile, shared over 90 percent of the market. In this and other oligopoly industries, a high degree of competition characterizes the market. Because both production and pricing decisions determine profit, the firms do not act in isolation. The firms act in a process of *strategic interdependence* by considering the behavior of their rivals.

From the perspective of the mobile network providers, it is in their best interest to maintain high prices. This way, each firm maximizes profit. But one firm may choose a different path, decrease the price, and gain market share. How will the other firms react? Most likely, they will also decrease the price. The reason is that they do not want to lose customers. The result is a process of mutual interdependence: the firms attempt to maximize profit but acknowledge the actions of their rivals.

Another example of an oligopoly market is the airline industry in the United States with American, Delta, Southwest, and United having more than 60 percent of the market share. The service is standardized but the firms have specific hubs. The market power of each firm is derived from the high barriers to entry into the

DOI: 10.4324/9781003533115-11

industry, such as the capital and branding requirements. Because a small number of large firms offer a majority of the airline routes, they act in a mutually interdependent manner. The output and pricing decisions of one firm impact the other airlines. When one firm offers a discounted fare, the others follow. While the firms have different cost structures, they compete with the number of passengers and departures.

The previous chapters explain that market structure is characterized in three ways: the number of sellers in the market, whether the product is standardized or differentiated, and if there are barriers that prevent firms from entering or leaving the industry. In oligopoly markets, a small number of large firms produce most of the output. The products may be standardized or differentiated. The differentiated products require advertising. Because each firm has a large degree of market power, significant barriers exist.

In addition to mobile network providers and airlines, the automotive, computer operating systems, oil, and steel industries operate as oligopoly markets. These industries are characterized by one dominant firm and a few followers or a small number of firms with similar market share. The point is that there are many examples of oligopoly markets, but the firms act in a process of mutual interdependence. To address these concepts, this chapter considers the definition of market power, how oligopolies emerge, oligopoly models, game theory, and applications of game theory.

DEFINING MARKET POWER

In specific industries, economists are interested in determining the concentration of output that comes from the largest firms. Two common methods exist: the *concentration ratio* and *Herfindahl–Hirschman Index (HHI)*. The concentration ratio of an industry consists of the market share of the four largest firms. While useful, this ratio may understate the role of a dominant firm. Table 9.1 provides an example. In Industry A, each firm has the same market share. Industry B has a dominant firm with 70 percent of the market. In the latter industry, the four largest firms produce all of the output, but the largest firm serves as the market leader. With the two industries, the concentration ratios are equal: the four largest firms provide 100 percent of the market. In the absence of additional information, however, this method does not reveal the difference

Table 9.1 Concentration ratios

	Industry A	Industry B
Firm 1	25%	70%
Firm 2	25%	10%
Firm 3	25%	10%
Firm 4	25%	10%

between the two industries. The dominant firm in Industry B has a larger market share.

The *HHI*—developed by two economists—addresses this shortcoming. In the United States, government institutions such as the Federal Trade Commission and the Department of Justice use the *HHI* to evaluate market power and the potential outcome of mergers and acquisitions. The index uses the following equation:

$$HHI = \left(s_1\right)^2 + \left(s_2\right)^2 + \ldots + \left(s_n\right)^2,$$

where s_1, s_2, ..., s_n are the percentage market shares for each firm in the industry. In applying the formula, the *HHI* calculates the sum of the squares of the market share of each firm. Higher values of the index demonstrate larger market concentrations, larger levels of market power, and lower levels of competitiveness. Lower values of the index demonstrate smaller market concentrations, smaller levels of market power, and higher levels of competitiveness. The range of numerical outcomes varies from zero (an industry with a huge number of small firms) to 10,000 (an industry with a monopoly). For Industry A, the *HHI* is calculated as follows:

$$\begin{aligned} HHI_A &= \left(25\right)^2 + \left(25\right)^2 + \left(25\right)^2 + \left(25\right)^2 \\ &= 625 + 625 + 625 + 625 \\ &= 2,500 \end{aligned}$$

For Industry B, the result is different:

$$\begin{aligned} HHI_B &= \left(70\right)^2 + \left(10\right)^2 + \left(10\right)^2 + \left(10\right)^2 \\ &= 4,900 + 100 + 100 + 100 \\ &= 5,200 \end{aligned}$$

These calculations demonstrate that Industry B has a firm with a large degree of market power. Industry A is therefore more competitive than Industry B.

The *HHI* has an important application. In 1992, the Federal Trade Commission and Department of Justice established merger guidelines:

- If the *HHI* < 1,000, the industry is not concentrated.
- If 1,000 < *HHI* < 1,800, the industry is moderately concentrated.
- If the *HHI* > 1,800, the industry is highly concentrated.

The rules are as follows: when the *HHI* < 1,000, mergers will be approved. If 1,000 < *HHI* < 1,800, mergers will be closely evaluated. If the *HHI* > 1,800, mergers are not approved. In both Industry A and Industry B, the firms would not be allowed to merge.

HOW OLIGOPOLY MARKETS EMERGE

In the long run, the firms in oligopoly markets may or may not earn an economic profit. The reason is that the output price may not exceed the *ATC* at the optimal level of production. But even when oligopolies earn an economic profit, it is difficult for new firms to enter the industry. In the airline and mobile network provider industries, a small number of large firms produce most of the output. Many reasons complicate the process of entry: the existence of high startup costs, difficulty in establishing a brand name, and problems in gaining market share. As a result, the emergence of oligopoly markets depends on the barriers to entry. These barriers— economies of scale, legal, reputation, and strategic—maintain the economic position of the firms in the industry, while minimizing the number of competitors.

ECONOMIES OF SCALE

Economies of scale refer to the range of production in which the average cost declines. When an efficient scale of production exists as a large percentage of the market, the oligopoly will achieve a lower *ATC* than a competitor. Because smaller firms struggle to establish this cost advantage, larger firms are in a better position to survive the competitive pressure. As a result, economists identify some oligopolies as *natural oligopolies*, similar to natural monopolies. A natural oligopoly exists when the number of firms that minimizes the TC of the industry is less than the highly competitive number of firms but greater than one. The airline and mobile network provider industries serve as examples.

LEGAL BARRIERS

Oligopoly markets often have legal barriers, such as copyrights, licensing requirements, and patents. In the pharmaceutical industry, for example, patents protect the ability of firms to bring certain drugs to the market. A patent gives the holder the exclusive right to develop, sell, or use an invention for a specific period of time. The patents help to determine why the pharmaceutical industry is an oligopoly. In this context, oligopolies often allocate resources to lobby the government to maintain their market status, maintain their tax status, limit foreign competition, establish zoning rules, and work to restrict market competition. The result of this lobbying effort is an increase in the ATC of production.

REPUTATION

Firms in oligopoly markets have well-established reputations. The consumers know their brand names, products, and market behavior. The consumers are familiar with the advertising and product choices. A firm's reputation creates an incumbency advantage, creating a barrier to entry for new firms. This familiarity holds true in the airline, mobile network provider, and other oligopoly industries. While an entrant may establish a brand name and gain market share, it requires a significant commitment to advertising. In the automobile industry, Tesla serves as an example, focusing on electric vehicles.

STRATEGIC BARRIERS

Oligopolies implement strategies that restrict potential competitors. They establish exclusive deals to be the sole suppliers of products. They maintain excess capacity to notify potential competitors that they have the ability to increase the production of output. They interact with their existing competitors in such a way as to maintain market share. They differentiate their products in order to identify and communicate the qualities of their brands. They maintain their consumer networks, enhancing the value of their products with the consumer base. Together, these strategic barriers complicate the process of firms entering the industry.

OLIGOPOLY MODELS

This book addresses four market structures: monopoly, oligopoly, monopolistic competition, and perfect competition. Of the four market structures, the oligopoly presents the biggest challenge for economists. The firms in the monopolistic, monopolistically competitive, and perfectly competitive industries act independently. Even though oligopolies attempt to maximize profit, they do not act independently of their competitors. They act in a strategically interdependent way.

Economists therefore analyze oligopolies in terms of their relationship with other firms in the industry. They develop oligopoly models. Consider the airline industry. If an airline lowers its price for a common route, its rivals follow. If an airline raises its price for a common route, its rivals do not follow.

To analyze oligopolies, economists study the process of strategic interdependence. When an oligopoly adjusts the price, how do the rivals respond? After the adjustment occurs, what characterizes the final market position of the firms? Two oligopoly models address these questions: the cartel model and the kinked demand model.

CARTEL MODEL

A *cartel* is a group of firms in an industry that agree to collude on quantity, price, and distribution. The world's most famous cartel, the Organization of the Petroleum Exporting Countries (*OPEC*), regulates the price of a barrel of oil for its members in order to influence the global price. The model includes firms that demonstrate collusive behavior, leading to a system of joint profit maximization. The assumption is that the firms collude to operate like a monopoly by raising the price and reducing the quantity of output relative to a competitive industry. In many areas, such as the European Union and the United States, collusion is illegal. If oligopolies in these areas want to collude, they must collude indirectly by observing the behavior of their rivals. But international law does not ban collusive behavior.

As shown in Figure 9.1, four firms form a cartel. In the cartel, they agree to produce at the profit-maximizing level of output for a monopoly where $MR = MC$ (40 units). The cartel restricts the level of output below the competitive level of 60 units (where MC = demand). The price set by the cartel is $80 per unit. At the profit-maximizing level of output of 40 units, each member of the cartel produces a fixed quota. If the quotas are the same, each of the four members produces 10 units of output, sharing the profit equally. The objective of the cartel is to maximize its market power, equal to a monopolist. By colluding, the members achieve the objective.

In a cartel, an incentive exists to cheat. A member may increase its share of the profit if it produces more than its quota. For example, if one member increases its production to 20 units, the cartel produces 50 units. The price falls from $80 to $70. In the process, the TR for the cartel decreases by $400 ($10 × 40 units), equal to the lighter shaded area. All of the members of the cartel experience a decrease in TR with each member losing $100. Given this shared loss, the member that cheats earns an additional $700 in revenue ($70 × 10 units), equal to the darker shaded area. The MR from cheating equals $700 − $100 = $600. As long as the MC of

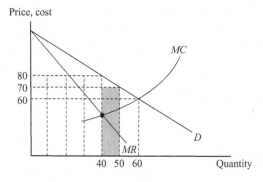

Figure 9.1 Cartel model

producing an extra ten units of output is less than $600, the choice makes sense for the cheater if the other members of the cartel do not respond.

The problem from the perspective of the cheating member, however, is that the other firms will respond. One option is to sanction the cheater by reducing its future production quota. But a second option is for the others to follow. As more members of the cartel increase the production of output beyond their quota, the price falls from $70 to the competitive level of $60, while the production increases from 50 units to 60 units. By reducing the level of the market power of the cartel, the outcome of a lower price and higher quantity benefits consumers.

This example demonstrates that market forces destabilize cartels. The members may not detect an increase in the production of output by a single country or firm. But when the members recognize that the cheater surpasses its quota, the effects on the cartel become more pronounced. If the *MC* of production is low, this reality increases the likelihood that the other members will lower the price. For *OPEC*, the *MC* of producing an additional barrel of oil is often as low as $10. At the competitive position where *MC* = demand, an additional unit of output generates $60 in revenue but costs $10. This economic reality provides the incentive to cheat. But if all members of the cartel decrease price and increase output, the cartel breaks down.

Even though an incentive exists for one member to cheat, several methods increase the stability of the group. First, the cartel may implement legal provisions that govern the production quotas. If a member exceeds its quota, the cartel may remove it from the group. Second, the cartel may restrict the number of members to those who share the goal of profit maximization. This way, the cartel decreases the likelihood of cheating. Third, the cartel has more stability if each member's cost structure is the same. In this situation, individual members do not have a cost advantage.

KINKED DEMAND MODEL

The model of kinked demand does not assume collusive behavior. The firms adjust the price in specific circumstances. Figure 9.2 presents two demand curves: D_1 and D_2.

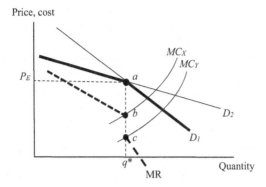

Figure 9.2 Kinked demand model

The demand curve D_1 represents the demand for one firm's output when all the other firms in the industry follow a change in price. Demand curve D_1 is less elastic (steeper) because when the firm raises the price and others follow, the quantity demanded decreases slowly as consumers do not have the option to substitute to lower-priced goods.

The demand curve D_2 represents the demand curve for one firm's output when all the other firms in the industry do not follow a change in price. Demand curve D_2 is more elastic (flatter) because when the firm raises the price and others do not follow, the quantity demanded decreases quickly as consumers switch to lower-priced goods of competitors.

Using this framework, the model of kinked demand has two assumptions:

- If a firm in an oligopoly market increases its price, the other firms do not follow. In this case, the other firms expect their market share to increase.
- If a firm in an oligopoly market decreases its price, the other firms follow. In this case, the other firms do not want to lose their market share.

The demand curve facing the firm is therefore the bold sections of demand curves D_1 and D_2. At point *a*, the demand curve is kinked. The relevant portion of the *MR* curve is drawn as dotted and bold from both D_1 and D_2. The discontinuity of space between points b and c means the MC varies between MC_X and MC_Y. Because MC passes through the discontinuity, the price (P_E) and quantity (q^*) prevail. The discontinuity establishes the model's price stability. The MC curve adjusts between points b and c before the firm has an incentive to alter price. This reality emphasizes the strategic interdependence.

GAME THEORY

Game theory is a method to study strategic choice, in which the outcome of a game depends on the choices of all of the players. Because oligopolies engage in strategic interdependence, it is an appropriate framework for this market structure. In the field of economics, game theory is used to study altruism, the behavior of firms, conflict, and many other topics. Game theory provides a way to analyze the interdependent choices of economic agents that lead to outcomes corresponding to the utilities of the agents. An important and interesting aspect of game theory is that the equilibrium may be suboptimal from the perspective of the players.

FRAMEWORK OF GAME THEORY

Game theory offers a method to conceptualize the strategic interaction between decision-makers. It involves rules, strategies, and payoffs. The rules provide the instructions that influence choices. The strategies are options for players in which the outcome depends on both the player's choice and the responses of other players. The payoffs are the values assigned to the outcome of a game, including monetary, psychological, and social payoffs. Together, the rules, strategies, and payoffs establish how a game is played. The actions of cooperation and defection approximate the choices of real-world situations.

LANGUAGE OF GAME THEORY

If a choice leads to the highest payoff, a *dominant strategy* exists. But a game's outcome may exist as a *noncooperative solution* when individuals do not engage in cooperative behavior and pursue their own self-interest. The Nash equilibrium—named after the mathematician and Nobel Laureate John Nash—exists as an outcome when players opt for their dominant strategies. Two common types of games are *extensive form games* and *strategic form games*. The extensive-form games describe the setting with a diagram of player choices. Because this form characterizes choices at different moments of time, it involves sequential games when players make their decisions in turn. Strategic form games describe the setting with a decision matrix. Individual players make decisions without knowing the choices of the other players. This form is common for simultaneous games when choices occur at the same time.

PRISONER'S DILEMMA

The most famous simultaneous game is the prisoner's dilemma. The idea is that two rational agents either cooperate for mutual benefit or betray each other for personal gain. Suppose Players *A* and *B* are suspected of a crime, taken into custody, and placed in different rooms. They cannot collaborate. The authorities have enough evidence to convict them of resisting arrest but suspect them of a more serious crime. Each player decides whether or not to confess (Figure 9.3).

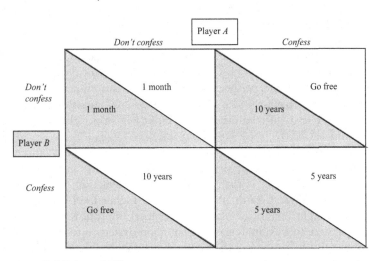

Figure 9.3 Prisoner's dilemma

The outcome is established in the following manner. If both of the players do not confess, they each receive a one-month sentence (top-left box). From the perspective of the players, this is the preferred outcome. But it is not the Nash equilibrium. Each player is tempted by an incentive to betray the other. If one player does not confess but the other does, the player who confesses goes free while the other receives a sentence of 10 years (top-right box or bottom-left box). Among rational players, this reality creates a doubt about the viability of the top-left box. As a result, for Player A, the rational choice is to confess regardless of what Player B does. For Player B, the rational choice is to confess regardless of what Player A does. Therefore, the Nash equilibrium is the bottom-right box: both players confess, receiving five-year sentences. Each player has a dominant strategy to confess, which determines the Nash equilibrium. From the perspective of the players, however, this rational outcome is suboptimal.

ECONOMIC APPLICATION OF GAME THEORY

Game theory establishes a context in which the payoffs depend on the choices of the players. With oligopolies, profit exists as the payoff. With two players in a duopoly game, the payoff matrix provides the incentive to choose one outcome or another. In Figure 9.4, Firms A and B choose between the production of 1,000 or 2,000 units of output.

The firms have different choices. If they collude and produce 1,000 units of output each, they maximize their joint profits (top-left box). From the perspective of the firms, this choice requires cooperative behavior. But if a firm produces 2,000 units of output, its profit rises while the other firm's profit falls (top-right box and bottom-left box).

In oligopoly industries, this incentive to cheat, produce more output, and gain market share exists as a short-term and myopic strategy. The reason is that, with strategic interaction, the other firm will follow. If both firms produce a higher level of output (bottom-right box), each earns a lower level of profit than if they cooperated. In a duopoly game, a common strategy is to start with cooperative behavior and then copy the choice of the other player if the strategy changes. From the perspective of the firms, however,

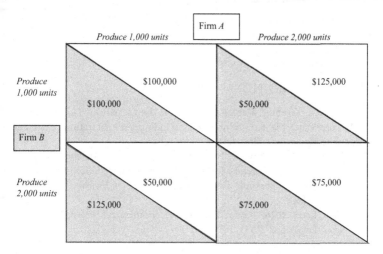

Figure 9.4 Duopoly game

the bottom-right box, although a Nash equilibrium, exists as a sub-optimal outcome.

The lesson of the duopoly game is that if oligopolists expect to compete with each other for a long period of time, they may decide that it's in their best interest to help other firms in the industry by restricting output and maximizing joint profits. But if the other firms change course and increase their output, the strategy changes. If the firms restrict output when collusion is illegal, *tacit collusion* occurs.

KEY TERMS

cartel
concentration ratio
dominant strategy
extensive form games
game theory
Herfindahl–Hirschman Index
natural oligopolies
noncooperative solution
oligopolies

strategic form games
strategic interdependence
tacit collusion

FURTHER READING

Berry, Steven, Gaynor, Martin and Morton, Fiona. 2019. "Do Increasing Markups Matter? Lessons from Empirical Industrial Organization." *Journal of Economic Perspectives*, 33(3): 44–68.

Crawford, Vincent. 2016. "New Directions for Modelling Strategic Behavior: Game-Theoretic Models of Communication, Coordination, and Cooperation in Economic Relationships." *Journal of Economic Perspectives*, 30(4): 131–150.

Samuelson, Larry. 2016. "Game Theory in Economics and Beyond." *Journal of Economic Perspectives*, 30(4): 107–130.

10

MONOPOLISTIC COMPETITION

DIFFERENTIATION OF PRODUCTS

In monopolistically competitive industries—characterized by a large number of sellers, differentiated products, and low barriers to entry and exit—the firms sell products that compete in the same market; however, the consumers do not view the products as perfect substitutes. With coffee shops, for example, Starbucks has served as the market leader with many other businesses vying for market share. The consumers in the market do not view the coffee from Starbucks as a perfect substitute for the coffee from Dunkin'. The consumers view the coffee from Starbucks as a differentiated product.

Starbucks implements several practices that achieve this outcome. It establishes a unique coffee experience, offers an efficient service, and supplies food items that complement coffee drinks. The company argues that it sells high-quality coffee, maintaining a close relationship with coffee suppliers. The company makes these choices to connect with customers.

To maintain market share, the competitors of Starbucks differentiate their products. Dunkin' competes with Starbucks, especially with respect to customer satisfaction. The company offers a brand of coffee that is considered by many customers as more cost effective when compared to Starbucks. The prices are considered to be more competitive. Dunkin' pairs the coffee with donuts and other breakfast items, emphasizing the bundling option. A distinct range of food and drinks targets specific audiences, including commuters, members of a neighborhood, and those with specific spending habits.

DOI: 10.4324/9781003533115-12

Firms with some market power such as Starbucks or Dunkin' set prices above the prices of perfectly competitive firms while maintaining market share. There is a segment of the consumer base that prefers the products of these firms and is willing to pay a small premium. The imperfect degree of substitutability between products means that firms with market power (even a small degree of market power for the firms in monopolistic competition) undertake a process of *product differentiation*. The firms establish a competitive advantage by increasing the willingness of consumers to buy their products. Each firm provides a product that is different from the products of its competitors. A differentiated product is a close substitute but not a perfect substitute for the output produced by other firms.

Product differentiation serves as a driving force in monopolistically competitive markets. The firms compete on the basis of *marketing* and quality. Marketing is the act of promoting and selling goods and services. Successful marketing campaigns increase the demand for output. The quality of a good or service consists of the attributes that make it different from other forms of output. The aspects of quality include aesthetics, durability, features, performance, and reliability. Given a market price, consumers choose a product with a higher level of quality when compared to other options.

Product differentiation also serves as a barrier to entry, but not an insurmountable barrier. In the model of monopolistic competition, firms may enter the industry. But the firms that enter must advertise, establish a brand name, and sell appealing products. These acts require a continuous allocation of resources for marketing, which increases the firm's ATC. In the market, some firms successfully differentiate their products, but others struggle to achieve this outcome. This market reality is the reason that some firms in monopolistic competition earn a profit or break even while others suffer losses and go out of business.

In addition to the coffee shop industry, many other monopolistically competitive industries exist, including clothing, groceries, hair salons, hotels, and restaurants. As this chapter explains, firms in monopolistically competitive industries face a downward-sloping demand curve. Each firm supplies a small percentage of the total output in the industry. As a result, the firms have a small degree of market power; however, they are highly competitive because it is possible for new firms to enter the market. As a result, the typical firm in monopolistic competition earns zero economic profit in the long run. That is, in the long run, it breaks even.

The market structure of monopolistic competition leads to benefits and costs. The benefits include the tendency of the firms to provide a variety of products and quality services. The result is that the consumers experience a wide range of choices. The costs include allocative and productive inefficiencies, a break-even position in the long run, and waste in the form of excessive packaging and marketing materials.

To address these topics, the chapter discusses the short-run model of monopolistic competition, the effects of firm entry on demand, product development and marketing, the long-run model, and the comparison between monopolistic competition and perfect competition.

SHORT-RUN MODEL OF MONOPOLISTIC COMPETITION

In the short run, both fixed and variable economic resources exist. The typical firm in monopolistic competition has a small degree of market power, resulting from product differentiation. As an example, suppose a locally owned coffee shop offers a variety of products, advertises on social media, and has loyal customers.

PROFIT SCENARIO

The coffee shop faces a downward-sloping demand curve for its food and drinks and a downward-sloping MR curve (Figure 10.1). Compared to a monopoly, the demand curve is relatively more elastic (flatter), reflecting the market competition. The monopolistically competitive firm chooses the optimal level of production (q^*) where $MR = MC$. In this case, $P > ATC_1$ at q^*, so the coffee shop earns a profit equal to the shaded area.

LOSS SCENARIO

In the short run, the high degree of competition means that the coffee shop may experience a loss over a certain period of time. Demand may be too low to generate an economic profit. The coffee shop may experience a slow season. Market conditions may

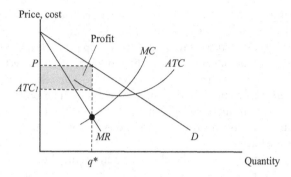

Figure 10.1 Economic profit for the firm in monopolistic competition

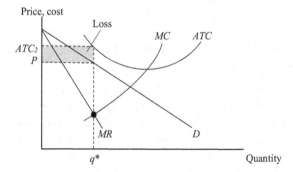

Figure 10.2 Loss for the firm in monopolistic competition

make consumers pessimistic about the future, discouraging them to spend money on coffee and complementary items. Other reasons may exist. A loss means that the price is less than the *ATC* at the optimal level of production. In Figure 10.2, the coffee shop chooses to produce at q^* where $MR = MC$. Because $P < ATC_2$ at q^*, the coffee shop is experiencing a loss equal to the shaded area.

COMPARISON BETWEEN MONOPOLISTIC COMPETITION AND MONOPOLY

When comparing the typical firm in monopolistic competition to a monopoly, both similarities and differences exist. With respect to the similarities, they both produce at the point where $MR = MC$. At this optimal level of production, they may earn a profit, experience a loss, or break even. They both charge the price that consumers are willing and able to pay, which is determined along the demand curve. With respect to the differences, the firms in monopolistic competition and the monopoly respond to their specific market structures. The main difference between the firms relates to the existence of a profit or loss. In the monopoly market, the barriers prevent additional firms from entering. As a result, the monopolist exists as the only firm in the market whether it is earning a profit or experiencing a loss. In contrast, if the typical firm in monopolistic competition earns a profit, the barriers to entry are not strong enough to prevent new firms from entering. If the typical coffee shop earns an economic profit, entrepreneurs will open new coffee shops, increasing the amount of output in the industry.

THE EFFECTS OF FIRM ENTRY ON DEMAND

If the typical firm in monopolistic competition earns a profit, more firms enter the industry. The barriers to entry are not significant enough to prohibit the process. Suppose as shown in Figure 10.3 that the initial demand curve facing the coffee shop is given by D. Although the ATC curve is not drawn on the graph, suppose a profit exists. When more firms enter the industry, two things happen to the demand curve. First, the demand curve decreases, shifting leftward from D to D_1. The MR shifts leftward from MR to MR_1. The coffee shop produces at q_1^* where $MR_1 = MC$. The

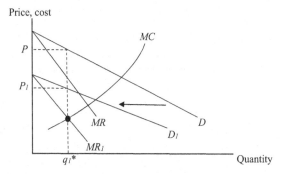

Figure 10.3 Firm entry decreases demand for the monopolistically competitive firm

decrease in demand leads to a lower level of production. Second, when more coffee shops enter the industry, the consumers have additional goods from which to choose. As a result, the demand curve becomes more elastic (flatter). Even though the consumers may demonstrate brand loyalty to the original coffee shop, the new competitors offer alternatives.

The leftward shift of the demand curve and movement to a more elastic position reflect the presence of new competitors. Even though the firms in this market structure recognize their competitors, they do not behave in the oligopolistic process of strategic interdependence. In monopolistically competitive industries with a large number of firms that sell related but differentiated products, the firms find the optimal level of production and set the price according to the demand curve. The firms in the industry may consider tacit collusion to establish a higher price. But the number of firms in monopolistic competition is large. Both coordination and collusion are not realistic.

Because the firms in the industry do not have a large level of market share, no one firm has the ability to establish the market price. Each firm faces its own demand curve. As a result, the actions of one firm do not affect the actions of the other firms. In the above example, the price decreases from P to P_1 when the demand curve shifts leftward. Given a cost structure, the result of a lower price is that the coffee shop experiences a movement toward break even.

PRODUCT DEVELOPMENT AND MARKETING

When making their output and pricing decisions, the monopolistically competitive firms allocate resources for product development and marketing. These allocations are necessary for product differentiation. They impact the production, pricing, and profit of the firm.

PRODUCT DEVELOPMENT

Both the high degree of competition and the prospect of new firms entering the industry motivate monopolistically competitive firms to develop new products. The idea is to transform an opportunity in the market into a new product for sale. This process entails all the stages of product development from the identification of a market need, establishment of an idea, valuation of an opportunity, creation of the product, release of the product, and update of the product according to customer feedback. Each step entails important decisions. For example, with the establishment of an idea, the firm must define the characteristics of the product, create the product attributes, and formulate its industrial design.

To maintain an economic profit, the firms allocate resources to product development or improve the products they have. They attempt to avoid the movement to a break-even position. A new or enhanced product that is differentiated from the competition attracts customers and establishes a demand curve that is less elastic (steeper), enabling the firm to increase both price and profit. In this respect, how a new product is developed differs across firms in the industry and within the same firm over time.

Although the imitators produce similar products, thus reducing the profit for the innovator, a first-mover advantage accrues to the firm that first introduces a new product. Depending on the economic circumstances and network effects—brand name, financial resources, and marketing skills—the first-mover advantage enhances brand recognition and customer loyalty before the competition arrives. When the competition reduces the profit for the innovator, the firm initiates the process of product development.

MARKETING

Marketing entails the promotion of goods and services. Successful marketing strategies include the creation of brand awareness, the establishment of optimal purchasing processes, and the generation of appropriate physical locations and digital platforms. The firms that differentiate their products ensure their customers are aware of their goods and services and perceive the businesses in positive ways. The objective of marketing strategies, an increase in demand, is reflected through sales data. If sales are strong, the additional revenue generated from marketing campaigns is weighed against the additional cost of advertising expenditures and other components of marketing.

In addition to establishing a link with demand, advertising both signals quality to consumers and establishes a brand name. A *signal* is a step taken by a firm to send a message to consumers about a good or service. A celebrity wearing an article of clothing or consuming a specific food item signals to consumers that they should also consume it. An important part of the process is that a signal does not need to convey product information if the advertising campaign is expensive and memorable. The establishment of a brand name links consumers with the products of specific firms. A brand name separates a firm from its competitors through identification and verification. The process of identification serves as a method of product differentiation. The process of verification authenticates a good or service as genuine or preferred. Together, signaling and establishing a brand name provide information about a product to consumers.

Firms in monopolistic competition incur ongoing marketing costs. As a result, a portion of the price that the buyers pay for a product is for marketing, including the cost of advertising. The result of the expenditure is to increase the firm's ATC curve.

The goal of advertising is to increase demand. By increasing product awareness and persuading consumers to switch to specific products, a firm forecasts a positive effect on demand. But the problem with monopolistic competition is the large number of firms in the industry. If a successful advertising campaign increases the demand for the products offered by a coffee shop, thus increasing its profit, more coffee shops will enter the industry. Over time, an increase in the number of coffee shops decreases the demand for the products from the original coffee shop. Consumers have more options. The new coffee shops will differentiate their products through advertising campaigns, bundling their food and drinks. In addition to an eventual decrease in demand for the original coffee shop that results from more competition, the demand curve becomes more elastic (flatter). As a result, advertising increases ATC but also decreases the price and resulting markup over cost. In the end, the firm must balance the generation of revenue against the cost of advertising.

LONG-RUN MODEL OF MONOPOLISTIC COMPETITION

The long-run model of monopolistic competition uses the easy entry/exit assumption of market behavior. If the typical firm is experiencing a loss, the market shrinks because firms will exit the industry. If the typical firm is earning a profit, the market will expand because firms will enter the industry. In both of these cases, the market is not in long-run equilibrium. Long-run equilibrium occurs when the profits or losses are eliminated.

How does the entry/exit assumption affect the economic position of the typical firm? Because the firms in the industry sell differentiated products, the process of entry or exit alters the demand curve for the typical firm. Two cases exist. First, if losses exist and firms exit, the demand curve for the typical firm increases, shifting to the right and becoming less elastic. At a given price, the coffee shops that remain sell more output. Second, if profit exists and firms enter, the demand curve for the typical firm decreases, shifting to the left and becoming more elastic. At a given price, the coffee shops that remain sell less output.

The long-run equilibrium occurs when entry and exit cease. This outcome exists when the firms in the industry earn zero economic profit. In the long run, a monopolistically competitive firm establishes a break-even position. At the optimal level of production, the firm covers its production costs, but nothing more. As shown in Figure 10.4, the demand curve is tangent to the ATC curve at q^*. This long-term, break-even position does not provide the incentive for firms to enter or exit the industry.

Firms in monopolistic competition attempt to avoid the movement to the long-run, break-even position. They differentiate their products, attempt to maintain or increase market share, provide

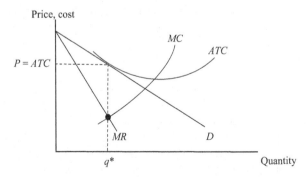

Figure 10.4 Long-run equilibrium in monopolistic competition

customer service, innovate, and act according to changing market conditions. They maintain their brand names and market positions and are willing to allocate a percentage of their operating budgets for product development and marketing. The firms in monopolistic competition attempt to maintain a profit as long as possible before moving to the break-even position.

COMPARING MONOPOLISTIC COMPETITION TO PERFECT COMPETITION

In many ways, monopolistic competition is similar to perfect competition. In both of the market structures, a large number of firms exist. Operating at the optimal level of production, the firms operate at a price that is equal to the ATC in the long run. Therefore, in the long run, the firms operate at the break-even position. The reason is that the firms in both of the market structures compete away the profits. In three ways, however, the market structures are different: product differentiation, the shape of demand, and efficiency.

PRODUCT DIFFERENTIATION

The product differentiation of the firms in monopolistic competition serves as an important contrast. Because Starbucks and Dunkin' differentiate their products, they compete in a monopolistically competitive market. These and the other firms in the industry allocate resources for product development and marketing. But perfectly competitive firms sell homogeneous products. They take the market price as a given, serving as price takers. As a result, they do not allocate resources for product differentiation.

SHAPE OF DEMAND

The shape of the demand curve serves as a second area in which monopolistic competition differs from perfect competition (Figure 10.5). Because perfectly competitive firms take the market price as given, they have a perfectly elastic (horizontal) demand curve. In the long run, the price (P_p) equals MC and the minimum ATC. But in monopolistic competition, the demand curve slopes downward. As a result, demand is not equal to MR. The monopolistically

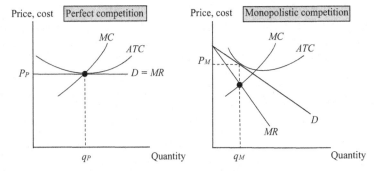

Figure 10.5 Monopolistic competition versus perfect competition

competitive firm sets a price (P_M) above MC. The price in monopolistic competition is higher than the price in perfect competition, all else equal. In addition, the quantity of output in monopolistic competition (q_M) is less than the quantity of output in perfect competition (q_P). The result of the lower price and higher quantity in perfect competition is more value for consumers. However, in monopolistic competition, the price is not that much higher and the quantity is not that much lower. Even though the consumers pay a higher price in monopolistic competition, they benefit from the variety and information that comes from product differentiation.

EFFICIENCY

Efficiency exists as the third area in which monopolistic competition differs from perfect competition. Recall the two forms of efficiency: allocative and productive efficiency. Allocative efficiency exists when the firm produces the output that consumers want. This efficiency condition exists if the price equals MC. Productive efficiency occurs when the firm produces output at the lowest cost. This efficiency condition exists if the price equals the minimum of ATC. In the long run, the perfectly competitive firm achieves both allocative and productive efficiency. This outcome means that the firm is making efficient choices, while the consumers benefit from competitive prices. The monopolistically competitive firm, however, achieves neither allocative nor productive efficiency. First, P_M is greater than MC, so MC pricing does not occur. This outcome means that the firm is not allocatively efficient. Second, P_M is greater than the minimum of ATC. This outcome means that the firm is not productively efficient. The reason that these two forms of efficiency are not met is that monopolistically competitive firms allocate resources for product development and marketing. Thus, they do not minimize cost.

EXCESS CAPACITY

In monopolistic competition, the firm produces q_M units of output, which is less than the quantity of output that minimizes ATC. Not only does this result mean the firm does not achieve productive efficiency but it creates *excess capacity*. Excess capacity occurs when the quantity of output that a firm could supply exceeds the demand for the output. When a firm produces a level of output that is less than its efficiency scale (which occurs when ATC is at a minimum), a firm has excess capacity. Because they produce at q_M, the firms in monopolistic competition have excess capacity. Because the firms in perfect competition produce at q_P, they do not have excess capacity.

Market conditions reflect this reality. Most of the time, gasoline stations have extra pumps available. Pizza places deliver their pizzas in less than 30 minutes. Most restaurants have extra tables in which they may seat more customers. If these firms lower their prices, they would increase their sales. But lower prices reduce profits. In this context, a *markup* is the amount by which a firm in an imperfectly competitive market raises the price above MC. A perfectly competitive firm does not implement a markup. A monopolistically competitive firm implements a markup equal to the difference between P_M and MC. Because of their market power, an oligopoly or monopoly establishes an even larger markup.

OUTCOME

The outcome is that monopolistically competitive firms do not achieve allocative or productive efficiency; however, the prices and output are not that different from perfectly competitive firms. Consumers value the product variety that exists in monopolistically competitive markets. The innovation in monopolistic competition leads to this outcome, but it comes with a cost. Advertising expenditures increase the ATC, while higher levels of competition decrease demand for the typical firm. Overall, the efficiency losses that result from product differentiation are offset by the competition and variety that exist in the market.

The structure of monopolistic competition leads to a wide range of products. Starbucks offers a large number of drink combinations. The idea is for consumers to specify their drink choices according to their tastes and preferences. Other firms establish a similar approach.

If too many varieties exist, however, the approach leads to wasteful duplication, another form of inefficiency. Do supermarkets need to offer dozens or hundreds of types of cereal? Do ice cream shops need to provide dozens of combinations? Does the market need such a large number of fast food places? One way to address these questions is to observe if consumer demand is sufficient to cover the cost of production. Then, the market supports a variety of products. But another way to answer the questions is that monopolistic competition decreases total surplus by creating inefficiency.

Which answer is correct? It depends on the circumstances. With fewer varieties, each firm sells more output, reducing the ATC. But then consumers have fewer products to choose from. In the end, the consumers benefit from the number of products in monopolistic competition. The value that consumers receive from product variety offsets the higher price.

KEY TERMS

excess capacity
marketing
markup
product differentiation
signal

FURTHER READING

Adams, Charles. 2021. "Quality-Differentiated Demand and the Analytics of Disruption." *The American Economist*, 66(2): 315–322.

Bronnenberg, Bart, Dube, Jean-Pierre, and Syverson, Chad. 2022. "Marketing Investment and Intangible Brand Capital." *Journal of Economic Perspectives*, 36(3): 53–74.

Wrenn, Mary. 2023. "Multi-Level Marketing: A Neoliberal Institution." *Journal of Economic Issues*, 57(4): 1043–1061.

PART III

LABOR, CAPITAL, AND FINANCIAL MARKETS

LABOR MARKET

The labor market for new college graduates is often challenging. As an example of a *factor market*, a market in which factors of production are bought and sold, a labor market brings together the supply of labor by individuals seeking jobs and the demand for labor by firms wanting to hire. Because they often lack full-time work experience, new college graduates often struggle to find stable, well-paying jobs. The market is competitive; so, many individuals apply for the same job. In addition, employers may require professional experience that new college graduates lack. The students who secure internships, demonstrate communication and problem-solving skills, and leverage professional networks help with the employment experience. But not all new college graduates have these opportunities. As a result of both supply-side and demand-side factors, younger members of the labor force, including new college graduates, normally experience a higher unemployment rate than their older and more experienced counterparts.

The production of output requires the employment of economic resources—the factors of production—including land, labor, capital, and entrepreneurship. This chapter analyzes the labor market. The production of educational, financial, legal, and medical services, for example, requires workers who are trained in their fields. Although it depends on the labor market, the students who want to enter these industries often need educational experiences beyond their undergraduate degrees. This reality increases the amount of time that they must stay in school or seek training, raising the cost of education. But the income from employment creates the incentive for supplying labor in these markets. Fortunately, many of the

DOI: 10.4324/9781003533115-14

tools in this book, including supply and demand, apply to the analysis of labor markets. The difference is that a labor market is an input market, while the supply and demand of goods and services occurs in output markets.

The markets for labor demonstrate different degrees of competitiveness. Competitive labor markets with a large number of firms demanding workers help to ensure fair wages. When the firms compete for workers and do not restrict labor mobility, the individuals have the opportunity of securing better work environments. In contrast, a concentrated labor market exists when a small number of firms hire most of the workers. In this situation, a lack of competition may lead to unequal levels of wage compensation and other forms of labor market discrimination. Other factors also impact labor markets, including unions and minimum wage laws. With respect to these and other issues, *labor economics* analyzes the structure of labor markets, incentives of labor market participants, and public policies.

In the study of labor economics, the economic perspective establishes a framework of analysis. Labor economics employs the theory of choice to address the behavior of economic agents, addressing several important questions. What gives laborers the incentive to work in certain forms of employment? Why do some individuals work more than others? Why do the firms in some industries employ fewer workers and more physical capital? Labor economics also analyzes labor market outcomes. Why do the workers in some industries receive higher wages? At what level of income do some laborers work less? When changes in the business cycle occur, why are some firms in a better position to adjust? To answer these and other questions, it is important to emphasize the assumptions of the economic perspective.

The assumptions include scarcity, opportunity cost, and adaptability. First, economic agents experience a scarcity of time. Individuals must decide how much time to devote to paid work or leisure. More time spent on paid work reduces the time for leisure. Second, because scarcity prevents economic agents from having everything they want, they must compare the costs of a choice with the expected benefits. The cost of additional work effort (less leisure) is the opportunity cost of working more. The benefit of working more is the additional money earned. When making the decision to engage in additional work effort, the individual must balance the costs and benefits. Third, labor market participants adjust to changing circumstances. A higher minimum wage encourages new workers to stay in their entry-level jobs for a longer period of time. When the demand for output increases, firms hire more workers. When the wages in a region increase, laborers move there seeking work. Many other changes in labor supply, labor demand, and policy alter labor market outcomes. In the discussion of the labor market in this chapter, these outcomes play an important role.

To address these issues, this chapter discusses labor supply, labor demand, equilibrium in the labor market, changes in equilibrium, and factors that impact the labor market, including economic discrimination, government policy, labor unions, and monopsony power. The chapter concludes with a discussion of the future of work.

LABOR SUPPLY

The decision to engage in paid work or leisure involves opportunity cost. When individuals pursue more leisure, they forgo additional work, reducing their income. The utility of these choices depends on the value assigned to both work effort and leisure. Economists often assume that individuals prefer leisure to work, although in the modern world, this valuation depends on the individual. Leisure establishes opportunities to exercise, read, spend time with friends, and engage in all other personal activities. But, in addition to generating income, paid work creates networks of social connections, a sense of personal satisfaction, experience in a field, and other benefits. The following discussion adopts the common practice in labor economics to divide the time of individuals between paid work and leisure. Leisure includes all activities that occur outside of the work environment, including household duties, interacting with friends, and pursuing hobbies.

The *supply of labor* is the time an individual is willing to spend working at different wage rates. At lower wage rates, the assumption is that individuals supply fewer hours of work per unit of time. At higher wage rates, individuals are willing to supply more hours of work per unit of time. But this direct relationship between the wage rate and work effort continues up to a certain point.

When the wage rate increases to where the individual is earning enough income to cover basic needs plus additional spending, individuals will substitute leisure for paid work as the wage rate continues to rise.

INDIVIDUAL LABOR SUPPLY

For an individual, the *backward-bending supply curve* demonstrates this reality (Figure 11.1). When the wage rate increases from W_1 to W_2, the amount of work effort increases from L_1 to L_2. The higher wage provides an incentive for the individual to work more. But the direct relationship between the wage rate and work effort continues to a specific point. When the wage rate increases from W_2 to W_3, the amount of work effort decreases from L_2 to L_1. In this range, the inverse relationship between the wage rate and work effort demonstrates that an increase in the wage rate provides the incentive for more leisure. What are the factors that determine the shape of the labor supply curve? For an individual, the relationship between the wage rate and work effort depends on two effects.

The *substitution effect* exists when individuals substitute work for leisure as the wage rate increases. They make this choice because the opportunity cost of leisure is rising. When the wage rate increases, individuals take advantage of the opportunity to earn more income. With respect to labor supply, the substitution effect is always positive. When the wage rate increases, the number of hours of work effort rises.

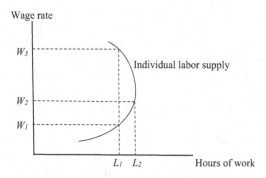

Figure 11.1 Individual backward-bending supply curve

The *income effect* refers to the fact that when the wage rate increases, income rises. When income rises, the individual has the opportunity to consume more goods, services, and leisure. As the wage rate increases to a level that provides a suitable lifestyle for the individual, an incentive exists to work less. The latter opportunity gives the individual the chance to enjoy more leisure. The income effect occurs when the individual chooses more leisure time when the wage increases beyond a certain level. With respect to labor supply, the income effect is normally negative, countering the substitution effect.

For the individual, the shape of the labor supply curve is a function of the two effects. When the substitution effect > income effect, the labor supply curve slopes upward. Because income is more important than leisure, a higher wage rate provides the incentive for the individual to choose more hours of work. When the substitution effect < income effect, the labor supply is backward-bending. Because income is less important than leisure, a higher wage rate does not provide the incentive for the individual to choose more hours of work. For workers in different industries, when does the backward-bending labor supply curve begin? It depends on the individual's preferences for work, income, and leisure. Normally, the backward-bending part of the labor supply curve exists at high levels of income. At this point, the income effect is stronger than the substitution effect. Most individuals choose more leisure when their incomes are beyond what they require to satisfy their basic needs.

MARKET LABOR SUPPLY

At the industry level, the market labor supply curve slopes upward. Higher wages attract more job inquiries and applicants. The positive slope contrasts with the slope of the individual labor supply curve, which is backward-bending. When the wage rate increases from W_1 to W_2 on the market labor supply curve, the quantity of labor supplied increases from L_1 to L_2. When the wage rate increases from W_2 to W_3 on the market labor supply curve, the quantity of labor supplied increases from L_2 to L_3. As a movement along the market labor supply curve, a higher wage rate leads to a larger quantity supplied.

LABOR DEMAND

The demand for labor is a derived demand. The demand for labor is derived from the demand for the output that it helps to produce. If the demand for an industry's output increases, firms in the industry demand more labor inputs. In the manufacturing sector, the production of more output requires more workers to participate in the production process. In the service sector, an increase in the demand for output requires more workers to satisfy the needs of consumers. Because the demand for labor is a derived demand, the strength of the demand for labor in an industry depends on two factors: the market value of output and the productivity of labor. If the market sets a high value for output, such as the games in a professional sports league, and specific players are highly productive, then the laborers will be compensated at high levels. Moving forward, it is important to emphasize that the immediate determinants of demand are the value of output and labor productivity.

THE HIRING DECISION

The firms use information on revenue and cost to decide how many workers to hire. Suppose a perfectly competitive market where the product price = $2. For a firm, the laborers demonstrate diminishing marginal returns (Table 11.1). When the firm hires more laborers, its level of total product (output) increases (column 2).

Table 11.1 Demand for labor in a perfectly competitive market

(1) Labor (L)	(2) Total product (Q)	(3) Marginal product (MP)	(4) Product price (P)	(5) Total revenue (TR = P × Q)	(6) Marginal revenue product (ΔTR/ΔL)	(7) Value of marginal product (MP × P)
5	30	–	2	60	–	–
6	54	24	2	108	48	48
7	72	18	2	144	36	36
8	84	12	2	168	24	24
9	90	6	2	180	12	12
10	92	2	2	184	4	4

The diminishing marginal returns exist because marginal product declines as the number of laborers rises (column 3).

When making the hiring decision, the firm balances the revenue with cost. On the revenue side, the firm calculates *marginal revenue product* (*MRP*), which is the change in *TR* when the firm hires one more worker (column 6). The firm determines the contribution of additional workers to *TR*. As the quantity of labor increases, the MRP decreases. On the cost side, the firm estimates the *marginal wage cost* (*MWC*), which is the change in the total wage cost when the firm hires an additional unit of labor. Two rules exist:

- When the *MRP* > *MWC*, the additional worker is adding more to the *TR* than to the *TC*. In this case, the firm increases profit by hiring more workers.
- When the *MRP* < *MWC*, the additional worker is adding more to the *TC* than to the *TR*. In this case, the firm increases profit by hiring fewer workers.

To maximize profit, the firm hires until *MRP* = *MWC*. Referring to Table 11.1, if the *MWC* equals $24 per hour, the firm hires eight workers, but not the ninth worker. If the wage rate equals $12 per hour, the firm hires nine workers, but not the tenth worker.

Another variable provides context. The *value of marginal product* (*VMP*) is the value to society generated by each additional laborer (column 7). It is determined by multiplying the marginal product by the price of output. In this example, the *VMP* = *MRP* because the market is perfectly competitive and the wage rate does not change. In an imperfectly competitive market, however, *VMP* ≠ *MRP* because the wage rate varies.

MARKET LABOR DEMAND

The market labor demand curve is the horizontal summation of the demand for labor from firms in the industry. It slopes downward, reflecting the fact that the quantity of labor demanded increases as the wage rate decreases, ceteris paribus. The market labor demand curve demonstrates how many workers all firms in the industry are willing to hire at different wage rates. The equilibrium wage rate that prevails in the market, however, depends on both the market labor supply curve and the market labor demand curve.

EQUILIBRIUM IN THE LABOR MARKET

The market labor supply and labor demand curves demonstrate the decisions of individuals to supply labor and firms to hire labor (Figure 11.2). On the supply side, the market labor supply curve shows a direct relationship between the quantity of labor supplied by individuals and the wage rate. On the demand side, the market labor demand curve shows an inverse relationship between the quantity of labor demanded by firms and the wage rate. Market equilibrium occurs when the market labor supply curve intersects the market labor demand curve, leading to the equilibrium wage ($24) per hour and the quantity of labor hired in the market (8,000 workers). At the equilibrium point, the labor market clears.

At a wage rate that is not equal to the equilibrium wage rate, however, the labor market does not clear. A point of disequilibrium exists. Given the market conditions, if the wage rate is above equilibrium, a *labor market surplus* exists. At $36 per hour, the quantity of labor supplied (9,000) > quantity of labor demanded (7,000). Compared to the equilibrium, additional workers are interested in supplying their labor services at a higher wage, but the firms do not want to hire at this amount. If the wage rate is below equilibrium, a *labor market shortage* exists. At $12 per hour, the quantity of labor demanded (9,000) > quantity of labor supplied (7,000). Compared to the equilibrium, fewer workers offer their labor services, while the firms want to hire more workers at lower wages. In both of these

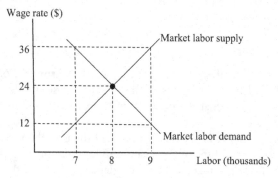

Figure 11.2 Labor market equilibrium

circumstances, an incentive exists for the wage to gravitate to equilibrium, thus eliminating the market imbalance.

CHANGES IN EQUILIBRIUM

There are several factors that cause the market labor supply and market labor demand curves to shift, creating a change in equilibrium price and quantity. On the supply side, the shift variables are demographic changes, nonmonetary aspects of work, nonwage income, and wages in alternative jobs. With demographic changes, an increase in the rate of immigration, labor force participation, or population growth cause the market labor supply curve to increase (shift to the right). If the nonmonetary aspects of work improve, such as the working conditions, the market labor supply curve increases. As nonwage income rises, including money from financial investments or trusts, the hours of work supplied decrease, shifting the market labor supply curve to the left. In many industries, the skills of workers transfer to other industries, such as computer programming and web design. If the wages increase in an alternative industry, the market supply of labor decreases in the industry under consideration. Figure 11.3 demonstrates that an increase in the market supply of labor from S_0 to S_1 decreases the equilibrium wage rate from W_0 to W_1 and increases the number of laborers working in the industry from L_0 to L_1.

On the demand side, the shift variables are changes in the prices of other economic resources, changes in product demand, and changes in productivity. If the prices of physical capital, such as

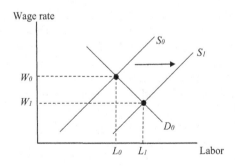

Figure 11.3 Increase in market labor supply

machines and equipment increase, the firms substitute labor for capital in new business activity, increasing the market labor demand. With an increase in the demand for products, the firms hire more workers, increasing market labor demand. With higher labor productivity, the demand for workers increases, shifting market labor demand to the right. An increase in the market demand for labor shifts the curve to the right, increases the wage rate, and increases the number of workers in the industry. A decrease in the market demand for labor shifts the curve to the left, decreases the wage rate, and decreases the number of workers in the industry.

FACTORS THAT IMPACT THE LABOR MARKET

The competitive market equilibrium demonstrates that firms hire workers at the equilibrium wage rate. In this context, all workers are treated equally. The discussion of the competitive labor market provides a useful framework of analysis, revealing the characteristics of market labor supply and market labor demand. But several factors alter the competitive solution, including economic discrimination, government policy, labor unions, and monopsony power.

ECONOMIC DISCRIMINATION

The presence of economic discrimination means that the preferences of consumers, employees, or employers elevate some workers over others, leading to wage differentials. A *wage differential* exists when two or more workers doing the same job make different wage rates. In this context, economic discrimination exists if laborers with the same level of productivity are treated differently. If workers with the same level of productivity receive different rewards, such as fringe benefits, opportunities for promotion, protection against layoffs, or wages, economic discrimination leads to unequal outcomes. An important implication of economic discrimination is the labor market outcome is both inefficient and unjust. For example, economic discrimination may lead to a *wage gap*, in which women are paid less on average than men for doing the same work. In labor markets, a wage gap may persist because of an employer bias, motherhood penalty, or a pattern of negotiation tactics. Economic discrimination creates imperfect labor markets.

GOVERNMENT POLICY

When markets function without government intervention, equilibrium prices and quantities establish market-clearing outcomes. But government policies may establish a price control in the labor market in the form of a price floor. With the establishment of a minimum wage above equilibrium, the equilibrium wage is considered too low from a social perspective. The implication of a minimum wage, however, is the creation of a surplus of labor. At the minimum wage, the quantity of labor supplied is greater than the quantity of labor demanded. In this case, the number of jobs that exist at the minimum wage is less than the number of laborers that want to work. The price floor decreases both consumer and producer surplus, leading to a deadweight loss and a movement away from the competitive position.

LABOR UNIONS

A *labor union* is a legal association of laborers that bargain over the terms of work, including wages and benefits. In labor unions, the members have a certain degree of market power. In the absence of a union, the laborers bargain over the terms of work. But union members bargain collectively, using strikes or the threat of strikes to achieve their goals. Workers organize unions according to craft, industry, or occupation. A craft union represents workers in a specific craft or occupation, such as teachers or truck drivers. An industrial union represents workers in a specific industry, such as auto workers or public sector employees. An occupational union represents laborers in specific lines of work, such as doctors or nurses. For its members, the benefits of a union are twofold: higher wages and collective bargaining. With the latter, the unions negotiate the contracts that determine benefits, compensation, health and safety policies, and hours. The costs of a labor union are the member dues and the fact that unions restrict the supply of labor to increase the wage.

MONOPSONY POWER

The buyers of labor may have the power to affect the wage. In the presence of monopsony power, one employer hires all of the workers in an industry and sets the wage. A *monopsonist* is a single buyer of an economic resource. By decreasing the demand for labor, a monopsonist reduces the wage. Examples of monopsony power include a single factory in a small town or a professional sports league that restricts player movement. Once a monopsony exists, imperfect competition leads to the reduction of marginal labor costs, increasing profit. In the labor market model, workers are paid wages that are less than the value of their marginal product, creating a disparity called the monopsonistic exploitation of labor. Compared to a competitive labor market, workers in a monopsonistic market are paid less. At the same time, monopsonistic employment is lower. The outcome of an imperfect labor market is a movement away from the competitive position.

THE FUTURE OF WORK

As the economy evolves, the labor market changes according to supply-side and demand-side conditions. An increase in the number of women in the labor market increases market labor supply. An increase in technology improves the efficiency of firms, altering market labor demand. A higher rate of two-income-earning households alters the work environment. These demographic and economic changes highlight several labor market trends, including the ability to work from home, file sharing and teleconferencing, and the growth of labor unions. The future of work includes the reality that many labor markets are tied to the process of globalization, the growing movement of goods, services, and economic resources across country borders. As globalization expands, global labor markets adjust according to global economic conditions. But many forms of work link to specific places, including bus drivers, electricians, and mechanics. In the industrialized economy, some trends will continue. A shift from manufacturing to services prioritizes human capital. The growth in both foreign direct investment and international trade leads to the outsourcing of labor-intensive forms of work. Artificial intelligence, the internet, and supercomputers alter the production process. Together, these factors influence the future of work by establishing new methods of supplying labor, enhancing human capabilities, and substituting labor with physical capital and technology.

KEY TERMS

backward-bending supply curve
factor market
income effect
labor economics
labor market shortage
labor market surplus
labor union
marginal revenue product
marginal wage cost
monopsonist
substitution effect
supply of labor
value of marginal product
wage differential
wage gap

FURTHER READING

Bhuller, Manudeep, Moene, Karl, Mogstad, Magne and Vestad, Ola. 2022. "Facts and Fantasies about Wage Setting and Collective Bargaining." *Journal of Economic Perspectives*, 36(40): 29–52.

Cassar, Lea and Meier, Stephan. 2018. "Nonmonetary Incentives and the Implications of Work as a Source of Meaning." *Journal of Economic Perspectives*, 32(3): 215–238.

Lavetti, Kurt. 2023. "Compensating Wage Differentials in Labor Markets: Empirical Challenges and Applications." *Journal of Economic Perspectives*, 37(3): 189–212.

Peri, Giovanni. 2016. "Immigrants, Productivity, and Labor Markets." *Journal of Economic Perspectives*, 30(4): 3–30.

CAPITAL AND FINANCIAL MARKETS

When students attend college, they give up the ability to earn more income in the present. The idea is to earn more in the future. During the educational experience, the decision involves either no income (if employment does not occur) or earning less than the total earning potential (if part-time work occurs). But the payoff from graduation is twofold. First, in many industries, college graduates have more employment opportunities. Second, higher levels of academic achievement correlate with higher lifetime earnings. As a result, the payoff from sacrificing current income is greater work and earning potential.

With economic decision-making, the question of whether to sacrifice in the present for a payoff in the future occurs on a regular basis. The question is important in many areas of economics, including business decisions, educational opportunities, and financial investments. For example, firms often consider whether or not to open a new business. In a monopolistically competitive industry such as fast food, opening a new branch in a specific market involves borrowing costs and upfront expenditures before revenues start to flow. Individuals often decide, moreover, whether or not to pursue extra education or training. In the field of economics, a certificate in data analytics or computer programming involves time, effort, and money, but the future payoff includes a greater potential for earning and a more diverse skill set. Finally, households often decide whether to save money. Additional saving in the present

DOI: 10.4324/9781003533115-15

decreases current consumption but leads to a higher level of future expenditure. In each of these cases, the decision-maker must evaluate whether a current cost is worth a future benefit.

To address this tradeoff, it is important to weigh present costs and future benefits. With present costs, this book provides a framework of analysis that includes the calculation of both fixed and variable costs. But this chapter discusses a method to calculate the present value (PV) of money that is received over time. With this method, it is possible to answer the question of whether a current sacrifice is worth a future payoff. As we will learn, this valuable tool applies to many circumstances. But the chapter focuses on two applications: capital markets and financial markets. The reason is that these markets are important in the area of microeconomics. They relate to the investment decisions and financial assets of firms. To address these issues, the chapter discusses physical capital and financial markets.

PHYSICAL CAPITAL

The production function demonstrates how a firm uses economic resources (land, labor, capital, and entrepreneurship) to produce output. There are two types of capital: human capital and physical capital. Human capital consists of the skills and training of members of the labor force. Physical capital is a tool in production that lasts a long time and is used to produce goods and services. Examples of the latter include the machines and equipment owned by firms. In this section, a focus on physical capital provides insight into the firm's investment decision.

MARGINAL ANALYSIS

The firm's decision to employ physical capital relates to profit maximization. Assume a firm must either buy physical capital or rent it at a constant price. In this framework, the firm's decision of how much physical capital to employ is similar to the decision of how much labor to employ. To demonstrate this concept, suppose a vendor in a market that is close to perfectly competitive operates a series of food trucks. The firm must decide the number of food trucks to operate in different neighborhoods.

To conceptualize the decision, the firm uses the marginal approach, forecasting whether an additional food truck will add more revenue to the firm than cost in a given period, such as a year. If the *MR* exceeds the *MC* for an additional food truck, the firm should make the purchasing decision. In this example, the *MRP* equals the additional revenue from one more food truck. The *MFC* is the additional cost of operating one more food truck. The profit-maximizing rule implies that the firm should operate an additional food truck as long as *MRP* > *MFC*.

Suppose first that the firm buys all of its food trucks. If a food truck costs $35,000 but lasts forever, the firm may buy the truck but forgo the opportunity to earn investment income with this money. The investment income serves as the opportunity cost. If the rate of return is ten percent, the firm could financially invest $35,000 and earn $3,500 in annual interest. In the process of profit maximization, this implicit cost is treated the same as an explicit cost. As a result, the *MFC* from purchasing a food truck is equal to $3,500 per year. If the *MRP* of one additional food truck exceeds $3,500 but the *MRP* of a second food truck is less than $3,500, the firm should purchase one additional food truck, but not two.

Suppose next that the firm rents all of its food trucks. If the rent on an additional truck equals $3,500 per year, the firm employs an additional food truck when the *MRP* > *MFC*. In sum, if the firm buys physical capital and it lasts forever or rents physical capital, the marginal approach provides a framework for analysis.

But this framework is limited. First, physical capital does not last forever. Over time, its value diminishes. Second, while a firm may rent physical capital, the economic resource is owned by some economic agent. While the firm in the example may rent an additional food truck, it must rent the food truck from a company that owns it.

To address these shortcomings, the following analysis assumes that firms buy their physical capital. The problem is that, while additional physical capital contributes to a future revenue stream, the revenue is not valued equally in the present. A new food truck may last ten years and generate revenue each year, but the revenue in the tenth year has a lower value in the present than the revenue in the first year. The next section explains why.

THE VALUE OF FUTURE REVENUE IN THE PRESENT

For economic agents, the PV of revenue received in the future depends on when the payment is received. Money put in the bank today earns interest over time. Money borrowed today requires interest payments over time. As a result of these realities, economic agents prefer to receive money earlier rather than later. Money received now has more value than money received in the future.

In this context, the value of future revenue is a question of PV, the value of a future payment in current money. Alternatively, the PV is the amount an economic agent would pay for the ability to receive a future payment. Suppose an individual must decide how much to pay to receive $1,000 one year from today. What should the individual offer? If the interest rate is five percent annually, the PV is the amount of money that would yield $1,000 in a year if lent at five percent interest. At five percent interest, the $1,000 would provide $1,050 in one year, so the PV is calculated in the following manner:

$$PV \times 1.05 = \$1,000.$$

Solving for PV yields:

$$PV = \frac{\$1,000}{1.05} = \$952.38.$$

If an individual lends $952.38 today at five percent interest, the individual would have $1,000 in one year. At this rate of interest, the individual would not give up more than $952.38 today for $1,000 in one year. That is, $952.38 is the PV of $1,000 in one year. Given a future value (FV) of money one year from today and an annual interest rate (r), the PV satisfies the following equation:

$$PV = \frac{FV}{\left(1+r\right)}$$

If the payment is received two years from today, the PV equation is:

$$PV = \frac{FV}{\left(1+r\right)^{2}}$$

In general, the PV of a payment received n years into the future is found in the following manner:

$$PV = \frac{FV}{\left(1+r\right)^n}$$

If the interest rate equals five percent, the PV of $1,000 received five years in the future is:

$$PV = \frac{\$1,000}{\left(1.05\right)^5} = \frac{\$1,000}{1.2763} = \$783.51.$$

Discounting is the act of converting a FV into a PV. In these examples, r serves as the *discount rate*, the rate used for the calculation of PV. In the absence of risk, the discount rate is the rate for borrowing and lending. In general, the PV is larger if the size of the future payment is larger, the interest rate is smaller, or the future payment occurs sooner rather than later.

Payments may occur at different future moments. Suppose an individual will receive $1,000 in one year, $900 in two years, and $800 in three years.

$$PV = \frac{\$1,000}{\left(1+0.05\right)} + \frac{\$900}{\left(1+0.05\right)^2} + \frac{\$800}{\left(1+0.05\right)^3}$$

$$= \$952.38 + \$816.32 + \$691.07$$

$$= \$2,459.77.$$

This amount, the total PV of the stream of payments, demonstrates why an economic agent who expects to receive money in the future must apply the discounting principle.

THE DEMAND FOR PHYSICAL CAPITAL

For a firm, the demand for physical capital depends on the relationship between the MRP and the marginal factor cost. Suppose in the food truck example that a new truck lasts ten years. But the revenue stream (MRP) differs (Table 12.1). Suppose the MRP of the first food truck equals $6,000. The MRP of the second food truck

Table 12.1 Present value of future income

Food truck	Additional annual revenue (MRP)	Total present value over 10 years
1	$6,000	$\dfrac{\$6,000}{(1+0.05)} + \dfrac{\$6,000}{(1+0.05)^2} + \ldots + \dfrac{\$6,000}{(1+0.05)^{10}} = \$46,330.41$
2	$5,000	$\dfrac{\$5,000}{(1+0.05)} + \dfrac{\$5,000}{(1+0.05)^2} + \ldots + \dfrac{\$5,000}{(1+0.05)^{10}} = \$38,608.67$
3	$4,000	$\dfrac{\$4,000}{(1+0.05)} + \dfrac{\$4,000}{(1+0.05)^2} + \ldots + \dfrac{\$4,000}{(1+0.05)^{10}} = \$30,886.94$

is $5,000. The third food truck generates $4,000 in *MRP*. For each food truck, the formula calculates the *PV*.

Because the cost of a food truck is given in today's money, the firm compares the *PV* of the future revenue stream with the current cost. If a new food truck costs $35,000, the firm should buy two additional food trucks: the firm gains more benefit in future revenue than cost. The *PV* of the future revenue stream for the third food truck equals $30,886.94, which is less than the cost. As a result, the firm should not buy the third food truck.

Even though this example focuses on food trucks, the *PV* principle applies to all forms of physical capital, including computers, equipment, and machines. With each decision, the first step is to calculate the total *PV* of the future revenue stream generated by the economic resource. This formulation serves as the *principle of asset valuation*. The second step is to compare the value in step one to the cost, determining whether the firm should purchase an additional unit of the economic resource. As the example demonstrates, the firm should buy an additional unit if the total *PV* of the future revenue stream exceeds the cost.

INVESTMENT DEMAND

In economics, *investment* occurs when a firm purchases additional units of physical capital. In the example, the firm is investing when it purchases an additional food truck. If the firm buys two food trucks, and the food trucks cost \$35,000, the firm's investment expenditure equals \$70,000 for the year. The example assumes an interest rate of five percent. At a higher interest rate, the future revenue streams have a lower PV for each year, so the total PV of each truck would be lower. At the same time, a lower interest rate would increase the PV of each year's revenue, so the total PV of each unit of physical capital would be higher.

Table 12.2 provides the total PV of the three food trucks at the interest rates of two percent, five percent, and eight percent. Compared to five percent, the total PV of the future revenue stream at two percent is higher for each food truck. At an interest rate of two percent, each PV of future revenue exceeds the cost of the food truck of \$35,000; therefore, at this interest rate, the firm should purchase three additional food trucks. Compared to five percent, the total PV of the future revenue stream at eight percent is lower for each food truck. At an interest rate of eight percent, the PV of the second and third trucks is less than the cost of \$35,000; therefore, at this interest rate, the firm should purchase one additional food truck.

This example demonstrates an important principle: a change in the interest rate alters the investment decision. The lower the interest rate, the more food trucks the firm will purchase, and the larger the investment expenditure during the year (Figure 12.1). The reason is that, even though the food trucks experience the same level of productivity at a lower interest rate, the future revenue from each food truck is worth more in today's dollars. But the cost is the same. As a result, with a lower interest rate, the firm demands more food trucks at a specific market price.

Table 12.2 Present value for different interest rates

Truck	Additional annual revenue (MRP)	Total present value with an interest rate of:		
		2%	5%	8%
1	\$6,000	\$53,895.51	\$46,330.41	\$40,260.49
2	\$5,000	\$44,912.93	\$38,608.67	\$33,550.41
3	\$4,000	\$35,930.34	\$30,886.94	\$26,840.33

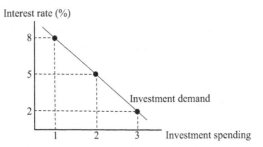

Figure 12.1 Investment demand

This concept applies to other forms of physical capital. When the interest rate decreases, firms purchase more physical capital. Specifically, as the interest rate decreases, firms apply the principle of asset valuation to assign a higher value to additional capital, choosing to purchase more. In the economy, a decrease in the interest rate leads to an increase in the quantity of investment expenditure.

SHIFTS IN INVESTMENT DEMAND

Although the investment decision is a function of the interest rate, other factors cause investment demand to change. These factors serve as shift variables for the investment demand curve:

- Capacity utilization—the percentage of the capital stock the firm is using. If capacity utilization is close to 100 percent, firms that want to produce more output increase investment demand, shifting the investment demand curve to the right.
- Cost of capital goods—the price of physical capital. As the price rises, investment demand falls, shifting the investment demand curve to the left.
- Economic activity—the amount of output produced in the economy. An increase in the production of output in the expansionary phase of the business cycle increases the demand for physical capital by firms, shifting the investment demand curve to the right.
- Expectations—the forecast for future sales. When expectations increase the forecasted return from investment, the investment demand curve increases, shifting to the right.

- Other factor costs—the price of other economic resources, including labor. If firms have the ability to substitute labor for capital in production, a decrease in the price of labor decreases investment, shifting the investment demand curve to the left.
- Public policy—rules and regulations that influence investment demand. If the government implements investment tax credits, the cost of capital decreases, shifting the investment demand curve to the right.
- Technological change—new methods to turn economic resources into output. When technological advance occurs, firms increase their demand for physical capital, shifting the investment demand curve to the right.

FINANCIAL MARKETS

The *financial markets* are markets in which money is transferred from economic agents who have excess funds to economic agents who demand the money. Financial markets increase economic efficiency by transmitting money from economic agents who do not have a productive use of it to the economic agents who do. Because of their role in this process of lending and borrowing, financial markets facilitate the process of economic growth. Financial markets include the supply of and demand for financial assets. Financial assets provide future income flows to their owners. As a result of the long lifespan of physical capital, firms often pay for their purchases of this economic resource by issuing and selling financial assets.

To expand production with capital investment, a firm may issue *bonds* (financial securities that provide interest payments to lenders for a specific period of time) or *stocks* (shares of ownership of a corporation, including a claim on the firm's assets and revenue). The process of issuing financial assets means the firm may generate money to use for the purchase of physical capital; however, it also creates an obligation for the firm to make payments to the holders of the financial assets. As a result, a link exists between the decision to invest in physical capital and supply financial assets. Whether or not the process exists as a profitable decision depends on the relationship between the cost of financial assets and the additional revenue from production.

To the owner of a financial asset, the stream of future revenue provides an incentive to purchase the asset. Economic agents calculate the value of a financial asset in the same way that they calculate the value of other assets, such as food trucks. They calculate the total PV of the future monetary payments that result from the ownership of the asset. As a result, the principle of asset valuation applies. With a financial asset, the PV of the future revenue stream serves as the asset's value.

STOCK MARKET

The principal way that firms raise money is through common stock. The company sells new shares of stock in the *primary stock market*. But the stocks are traded in the *secondary stock market*. The company that issues the shares of stock is not involved in the secondary market. But the secondary market is important because financial investors know they can sell their stocks. In addition, the stock prices in the secondary market influence the initial prices set for the primary market.

Economic agents hold stocks to diversify their financial portfolios, earn a rate of return, and have ownership shares. The ownership provides the stockholders with a series of rights, including the right to receive *dividends* (payments made to stockholders) and the right to vote for board members. The board sets the level of the dividends, recommended by management. At any time, the stockholder has the right to sell the shares of stock in the secondary market.

The current price of a share of stock (P_0) is calculated with the PV of all future cash flows. The cash flow includes the dividends in period i (D_i) and the selling price in period i (P_i). The interest rate is the required return on financial investments in equity (k_e), another term for stocks. With respect to the latter, k_e is the minimum amount of money that financial investors will seek or receive when they purchase company stock. Suppose the financial investor seeks a seven percent annual return, identifies a \$0.20 annual dividend, and forecasts a stock price equal to \$100 in one year. The following equation computes the current stock price (P_0) or PV of the future cash flow for a one-year time horizon:

$$P_0 = \frac{D_1}{\left(1+k_e\right)} + \frac{P_1}{\left(1+k_e\right)}$$

$$= \frac{\$0.20}{\left(1+0.07\right)} + \frac{\$100}{\left(1+0.07\right)}$$

$$= \$0.19 + \$93.46 = \$93.65.$$

This *PV* of the cash flow during the year equals $93.65. If the actual stock price set by the market is less than or equal to this amount, the financial investor should buy the stock. If the actual market price is higher, the purchase should not occur. The calculation of the current stock price in this analysis depends on the future expectations of dividends and the selling price. The *theory of rational expectations* assumes that economic agents form expectations identical to their optimal forecasts, using all available information. While this theory equates a rational expectation with an optimal forecast, an economic agent's prediction using the theory may not yield an accurate result. It may be impossible to forecast a future dividend or selling price. Economic conditions may change. The stock market may act in a volatile manner. As a result, the equation provides a method to compare the *PV* with the actual stock price, but an economic agent must consider that economic conditions may change.

BOND MARKET

A bond is a security in which a financial investor lends money to a company for a certain period of time. In return, the financial investor receives the face value of the bond or principal at a future maturity date plus regular interest payments. The effective annual interest rate of a bond is the *yield*. Newly issued bonds occur in the primary market. When a bond is sold, the transaction occurs in the secondary market. Even though the issuers of new bonds do not participate in secondary markets, this market affects the primary market. Two reasons exist. First, if the price of a bond decreases in the secondary market, the price of a newly issued bond will also decrease. Second, in the secondary market, if a bond's yield rises, the yield of bonds in the primary market will also rise.

Although bonds are often issued in denominations of $1,000, they may range in value between $50 and $10,000. The maturity dates of bonds are more than ten years, commonly 30 years. Bills and notes, other types of securities, range between a few months and ten years. A typical 30-year, $10,000 bond will make an annual coupon payment, such as $500, and then pay the $10,000 principal at maturity.

Suppose a discount security pays $10,000 in one year. To determine the market value, calculate PV. If the interest rate is five percent, the PV is:

$$PV = \frac{FV}{\left(1+r\right)^{n}} = \frac{\$10,000}{\left(1+0.05\right)} = \$9,523.81.$$

Because the PV is the amount of money the financial investor receives in one year, the PV is the total willingness to pay. At the same time, the PV is the lowest price at which the issuer is willing to sell.

An important principle is that the prices and yields move in opposite directions. The lower the price, the higher the yield. To demonstrate this inverse relationship, suppose a financial investor buys the security for $9,523.81. At the end of the year, the financial investor earns interest of $10,000 − $9,523.81 = $476.19. The annual yield is $476.19/$9,523.81 = 0.0499 or 4.99 percent. But suppose the market sets a price of $9,400. Then the interest is $10,000 − $9,400 = $600. The annual yield is $600/$9,400 = 0.0638 or 6.38 percent. When the price decreases, the yield increases. The idea is that financial security makes payments at fixed future dates. The lower the price for those future payments, the higher the rate of return or yield.

The bond price is determined by the forces of supply and demand. At a specific time, a certain quantity of bonds exists, no matter the price. In the market, the intersection of a vertical supply curve and a downward-sloping demand curve establishes the equilibrium price. A change in the bond price occurs, but the supply curve does not shift as often as the demand curve. The demand curve may shift because of changes in the attractiveness of other assets, the interest rate, and risk. For example, if stocks become less appealing, the demand for bonds increases and the price rises. If the interest rate increases, the PV declines, decreasing both the demand for bonds and the price. If a decrease occurs in the perceived level of risk, an increase in demand occurs, raising the price. Together, these factors alter market conditions.

KEY TERMS

bonds
discounting
discount rate
dividends
financial markets
investment
marginal factor cost
present value
primary stock market
principle of asset valuation
secondary stock market
stocks
theory of rational expectations
yield

FURTHER READING

Baranes, Avraham and Hake, Eric. 2018. "The Institutionalist Theory of Capital in the Modern Business Enterprise." *Journal of Economic Issues*, 52(2): 430–437.

Daniel, Kent and Hirshleifer, David. 2015. "Overconfident Investors, Predictable Returns, and Excessive Trading." *Journal of Economic Perspectives*, 29(4): 61–88.

GLOSSARY

advertising   the act of calling attention to goods or services in the market

aggregation   summation of individual market transactions

allocative efficiency   when firms produce the output that consumers want

antitrust policy   regulation that promotes competition

asymmetric information   when one party has more information than another party

average cost   the cost per unit of output

average fixed cost   the fixed cost of production divided by the quantity of output

average tax rate   value of taxes paid divided by the value of the base

average total cost   the total cost of production divided by the quantity of output

average variable cost   the variable cost of production divided by the quantity of output

backward-bending supply curve   when a higher wage entices laborers to work less

behavioral economics   method of analysis that uses psychology to explain decision-making

bonds   financial securities that provide interest payments to lenders for a specific period of time

budget constraint   goods and services a consumer may purchase with a budget

budget line   combinations of two goods that a consumer may purchase, given income and prices

cartel   group of firms in an industry that agree to collude on quantity, price, and distribution

ceteris paribus   all else being equal

choice   assigning values to different options

complements   goods consumed together

concentration ratio   market share of the four largest firms in an industry

consumer surplus   difference between what consumers are willing to pay and market price

consumer theory   area of microeconomics that addresses how individuals spend their money

copyrights   rights to film, perform, print, publish, or record an artistic, literary, or musical piece

corporation   organization authorized to act as a single entity

cross price elasticity of demand   change in demand for good x when price of good y changes

demand   maximum amount of output consumers are willing and able to buy at different prices

demand curve   graph that shows the relationship between price and quantity demanded

demand schedule   table that shows the relationship between price and quantity demanded

deadweight loss   cost to society of market inefficiency

diminishing marginal returns   decreasing marginal output as a single economic factor increases

discounting   act of converting a future value into a present value

discount rate   the rate used for the calculation of present value

dividends   payments made to stockholders

division of labor   when workers focus their skills and talent on specific areas of production

dominant strategy   best strategy no matter the choices of the other player

economic resources   factors of production that are used to produce output

economies of scale   average cost decreases when output increases

efficiency   allocating economic resources in an optimal manner

elasticity   degree of responsiveness of one variable to a change in another variable

equilibrium   state in which market supply and market demand are in balance

equity   fairness

excess capacity   when the output a firm could supply exceeds the demand for the output

extensive form games   sequential games when players make their decisions in turn

externality   external cost or benefit to individuals not involved in economic activity

factor market   a market for an economic resource

financial markets   transfer money from lenders to borrowers

firms   institutions that employ economic resources to produce goods and services

franchises   government authorizations for an economic activity

free riders   individuals who benefit but do not share the cost

game theory   method to study strategic choice

government failure   inefficiency caused by government intervention

government intervention   action by the public sector that seeks to alter economic decisions

Herfindahl–Hirschman Index   measure of market concentration to determine competitiveness

hyperbolic discounting   when individuals value immediate payoffs more than future payoffs

imperfectly competitive markets   markets that are less competitive than perfect competition

incentives   things that encourage economic agents to make a specific choice

increasing marginal returns   increasing marginal output as a single economic factor increases

industry   group of firms that are related due to their economic activities

income effect   when the wage rate increases, income rises

income elasticity of demand   change in demand from a change in income

inferior goods   when income increases, demand for these goods decreases

investment   when a firm purchases additional units of physical capital

labor   factor of production that focuses on the work that individuals do

labor economics   study of the labor force as an aspect of production

labor market shortage   quantity of labor demanded is greater than quantity of labor supplied

labor market surplus   quantity of labor supplied is greater than quantity of labor demanded

labor union   legal association of laborers that bargain over the terms of work

laissez–faire   free from intervention

land   factor of production that includes natural resources and geographic space

Law of Demand   when price increases, quantity demanded decreases, ceteris paribus

Law of Supply   when price increases, quantity supplied increases, ceteris paribus

long run   when all economic resources are variable

luxury   good that is a nonessential purchase

marginal cost   the additional cost from producing one more unit of output

marginal factor cost   additional cost from operating one more unit

marginal product of labor   change in output from one more unit of labor

marginal revenue product   change in total revenue when the firm hires one more worker

marginal tax rate   additional taxes paid divided by the change in value of the tax base

marginal utility   satisfaction from an additional unit of consumption

marginal wage cost   change in the total wage cost when the firm hires an additional unit of labor

market   mechanism that brings buyers and sellers together for the purpose of exchange

marketing   act of promoting and selling goods and services

market economy   using market forces of supply and demand to produce output

market failure   inefficient allocation of goods and services

market power   firm's ability to manipulate market price

market structure   industry classification that is determined by specific characteristics

markup   amount by which a firm raises the price above marginal cost

microeconomics   study of economic agents such as consumers and firms

mixed economy   form of economic organization with free markets and government intervention

monopoly   market structure with a single seller and no close substitutes

monopsonist   single buyer of an economic resource

natural monopolies   markets where one firm sells output at a lower cost than competitors

natural oligopolies   number of firms that minimize total cost is less than the competitive number

necessity   normal good that consumers buy regardless of a change in income

noncooperative solution   individuals do not engage in cooperative behavior

nonexclusive   cannot exclude individuals from using specific goods or services

nonrival   consumption by one person does not reduce the amount available to others

normal goods   when income increases, demand for these goods increases

normal profit   when total cost equals total revenue

normative analysis   use of value judgments such as what ought to be

oligopolies   when a small number of large firms produces most of the industry's output

opportunity cost   value of the best foregone alternative

partnership   arrangement by two or more parties to manage a firm and share its profits

patents   when government grants a property right to an inventor of a new idea, process, or product

perfectly competitive markets   markets with many buyers and sellers, who serve as price takers

physical capital   tangible objects that are used to make other things

positive analysis   use of objective thinking such as what is

present value   the value of a future payment in current money

price ceiling   maximum legal price

price controls   government-mandated maximum or minimum prices

price discrimination   selling the same product to different customers for different prices

price elasticity of demand   sensitivity of consumers to a change in price

price elasticity of supply   sensitivity of producers to a change in price

price floor   minimum legal price

price taker   when a firm accepts the market price

primary stock market   where newly-issued stocks are bought and sold

principle of asset valuation   calculation of the total present value of a future revenue stream

producer surplus   difference between market price and what sellers are willing to charge

product differentiation   strategy to encourage consumers to choose one product over another

production function   relationship between economic resources and the amount of output

productive efficiency   when firms produce output at the lowest cost

progressive tax rate structure   when the tax base rises, the average tax rate increases

property rights   authority to determine how an economic resource is used

proportional tax rate structure   when the tax base changes, the average tax rate does not change

public goods   output that is nonexclusive and nonrival in consumption

regressive tax rate structure   when the tax base rises, the average tax rate decreases

relative price   the price of one product measured in comparison to the price of another product

rent seeking   enhancing a firm's economic position without contributing to productivity

scarcity   limited supply results in a mismatch between supply and demand

secondary stock market   where financial investors buy and sell stocks

shortage   when quantity demanded is greater than quantity supplied at a price below equilibrium

short run when at least one economic resource is fixed

shutdown rule a firm should shut down if price is less than average variable cost

signal step taken by a firm to send a message to consumers about a good or service

sole proprietorship institution owned by one person with no distinction between owner and entity

specialization when firms organize the economic tasks so that the workers specialize

stocks shares of ownership of a corporation

strategic form games players make decisions without knowing the choices of the other players

strategic interdependence one player's outcome depends on the decisions of the other player

substitutes goods that are consumed instead of one another

substitution effect when individuals substitute work for leisure as the wage rate increases

sunk cost fallacy when individuals don't cancel an activity because they've invested money in it

supply maximum amount of output sellers are willing and able to sell at different prices

supply curve graph that shows the relationship between price and quantity supplied

supply of labor time an individual is willing to spend working at different wage rates

supply schedule table of numbers that shows the relationship between price and quantity supplied

surplus when quantity supplied is greater than quantity demanded at a price above equilibrium

systematic bias methodological deviation from an actual decision

tacit collusion when firms restrict output when collusion is illegal

technology method in which a firm turns economic resources into output

theory of rational expectations economic agents form expectations identical to optimal forecasts

total cost all of the costs of production

total product total amount of output a firm produces in a given period

total utility   level of satisfaction from the consumption of goods and services

trade   voluntary exchange of goods and services between economic agents

tradeoffs   when making a choice means giving up something else

utility   satisfaction

utility maximizing rule   equating the marginal utility per price for all consumption items

value of marginal product   value to society generated by each additional laborer

wage differential   when two or more workers doing the same job make different wage rates

wage gap   when women are paid less on average than men for doing the same work

willingness-to-pay   maximum price a consumer will pay for a good or service

x-inefficiency   when firms lack the incentive to control costs

yield   effective annual interest rate of a bond

INDEX

Printed in the United States
by Baker & Taylor Publisher Services